Cognitive Psychodynamics

Cognitive Psychodynamics

FROM CONFLICT TO CHARACTER

MARDI J. HOROWITZ

JOHN WILEY & SONS, INC.

New York • Chichester • Weinheim • Brisbane • Singapore • Toronto

Copyright © 1998 by Mardi J. Horowitz. All rights reserved.
Published by John Wiley & Sons, Inc.
Published simultaneously in Canada.

This publication is designed to provide accurate and authoritative information in regard to the subject matter covered. It is sold with the understanding that the publisher is not engaged in rendering professional services. If legal, accounting, medical, psychological or any other expert assistance is required, the services of a competent professional person should be sought.

Library of Congress Cataloging-in-Publication Data
Horowitz, Mardi Jon. 1934–
  Cognitive psychodynamics : conflict to character / Mardi J.
Horowitz.
    p. cm.
  Includes bibliographical references and index.
  ISBN 0-471-11772-2 (cloth : alk. paper)
  1. Psychoanalysis. 2. Identity (Psychology) 3. Interpersonal
relations. 4. Character. I. Title.
BF173.H7629 1998
150.19′5—dc21   98-5925
                                                       CIP

Printed in the United States of America.

10 9 8 7 6 5 4 3 2 1

For Carol, with love

Contents

Introduction

L IVING WELL requires passion, resilience to challenges, and a reasoned, morally tenable maintenance of commitments. These aims are difficult to balance, but that is the human condition. This condition includes living in distress due to emotional conflicts.

Mental and emotional conflict often involves severe contradictions in beliefs about personal identity and the discrepancy between existing and desired affiliations with others. Any study of psychology about character and personality must address these topics. Moreover, it must deal with unconscious mental processes and enduring (but slowly changing) structures of personal meaning. This book addresses these topics in a new way that integrates previous cognitive and psychodynamic approaches.

The central theoretical constructs are states of mind, defensive control processes (as used to regulate emotion), and person schemas. Person schemas are cognitive maps, often ones with a potential for high relational emotionality, that organize patterns of relationships and identity. They organize the complex balance between self-serving and "we"-serving aims so often called "character."

Empirical research on the reliability of operational definitions and the validity of these constructs has occurred since the publication of an earlier work on these topics titled *Introduction to Psychodynamics: A New Synthesis* (Horowitz 1988b). The present text builds on this research base.

Many in the field want a synthesis of concepts and a common language. Although complexity must be included, for the mind is quite complex, the integrative theory should be presented in a language accessible to all mental health clinicians, behavioral scientists, and intelligent readers interested in psychosocial meanings. For that reason, this text does not use traditional psychoanalytic terms such as *cathexis, id-ego-superego, libidinal* and *aggressive drives*, and *the repressed*.

During the early part of the twentieth century psychoanalytic theory did address vital, but often unconscious, psychological conflicts between moral codes, passions, and defensive distortions of reality. Major phenomena of psychopathology were very well described. Efforts to say how symptoms formed were more speculative. Although valuable insights were gained, the emergent explanatory theory was problematic. It was couched in a special language. Contemporary continuation of that early psychoanalytic language makes the theory hard to access in neighboring disciplines. Currently, new explanations of psychological symptoms and personality problems have evolved through cognitive sciences. It is useful to revise psychoanalytic language and present modern psychodynamics in a common language.

This book first presents basic concepts and then uses them as it explores the origins of identity, relationships, and character. It builds from the theory of person schemas, which evolved in a research collaboration between workers from different theoretical domains. This work first appeared in book form as *Person Schemas and Maladaptive Interpersonal Patterns* (Horowitz, 1991). In pragmatic terms, this theory is now used to answer questions such as how people form meaningful identities during development. And the character question—how people deal with the conflict between self-striving and their responsibility to others.

The theory of person schemas leads to an understanding of how beliefs are aggregated into useful packages of information and why passionate beliefs lead to a variety of emotional or defensive states. The language used to describe the organization of ideas and feelings into larger systems of meaning has to be psychosocial rather than neurobiological. This is not to deny the scientific fact that electrochemical exchanges, synaptic networks, and system integrations in the brain are the biological substrates for the involved associations between bits of meaning. Changes in neurons and transmitter substances make conscious and unconscious mental processing possible. However, for the purposes of the present discussion, the exact anatomy, physiology, and electrochemistry need not be examined. In that sense, this text is "substrate neutral." The focus of attention is on the meanings that these substrates produce. The mind/brain linking assumption is that the psychological meanings can be understood in the same way as neuronal functions: small systems for handling information combine to form larger systems, with feedback and feedforward between the nesting systems.

The approach used here starts with smaller systems of representation of ideas and feelings and builds toward larger systems that can answer complex questions such as what identity is, what the basis of attachments to others is, and why maladaptive relationship cycles repeat despite their poor results. Any attempt to answer these questions must consider why motives compete within the individual mind, as well as how they do so at both conscious and nonconscious levels. And it must address important concepts of change, such as how people become self-aware, how enhanced awareness can lead to insight, and how insight can lead to the many new decisions that can alter fundamental attitudes and lead to adaptive changes in behavioral patterns.

Thus, the focus of this book is on ideas and feelings. It seeks to explain the irrationality that often shows up in repeated relationships. The goal of such theory is to explain how ideas and feelings can be modified by heightened conscious awareness, formation of new insights, and making new decisions. To meet this goal and to start with episodes of directly knowable experiences, this book begins with episodes of awareness that signal the presence of strong emotional conflict. Episodes of such awareness are then considered as organized units of experience called *states of mind*. The utility of this procedure is described in *States of Mind: Configurational Analysis of Individual Personality* (Horowitz, 1979b, 1987). The term *configuration* refers there, as in this text, to multiple views of self and others (cognitive person schemas) and wishful, fearful, and defensive combinations of these views (psychodynamic formulations) (Erikson, 1954; Perry, Cooper, & Michels, 1987). Research has shown the validity of approaching individual formulation using such an integrative approach (Beck, 1976; Beitman, Goldfried & Norcross, 1989; Goldfried, 1996; Horowitz, 1991a, 1997b).

Analysis of states and cycles is used as an experience-close way of defining the phenomena to be examined. The explanations of how and why states occur then lead to a deeper understanding of emotion and motivation. Dilemmas of how to satisfy wishes while avoiding threats and fears are described in terms of desired and dreaded states, and states that function as defensive compromises. Subsequent chapters proceed from this platform of consciously known motivation (of wanting to defend against dreaded states while striving to achieve desired states). These explanatory chapters discuss how unconscious mental processes reconstruct beliefs, how associations of emotional beliefs lead to moods, and how information processing using self–other organizations such as role-relationship models influence social transactions.

In the contemporary debate between brand names of psychotherapy, unconscious defensive operations are a key issue. The psychoanalytic theory of repression is being severely challenged on scientific grounds. An alternate theory, that of dissociation, has been put forward to correct gaps in those explanations (Spiegel, 1994). Recovered memories, false memories, and unconscious fantasies are all subjects of renewed concern (Erdelyi, 1997), largely because these topics have entered the arena of tort law. To understand conscious awareness effectively, the issue of unconscious defensiveness requires a new theory.

This book proposes that unconscious processes include complex computations that allow people to anticipate where thought and action are going, and that unconscious cognitive control processes (as well as consciously volitional ones) can be used to stifle emotion (to avoid entry into dreaded states of mind). The concepts of control processes presented in this text evolved from careful attention to phases of defensive denial and intrusive (or breakthrough) thinking that increase after traumatic experiences, as defined in *Stress Response Syndromes* (Horowitz, 1977b, 1986; 1997b). The control process theory provides new categorizations that transcend psychoanalytic definitions of defense mechanisms. These defensive control processes account for how phenomena such as repression, dissociation, and projection are achieved by cognition.

The first half of this book provides a basic theory and language. It explains some clinical psychiatric symptoms that have high relevance for mental health professionals, especially psychotherapists. The second half of the book uses this theory and language to conceptualize development, endurance, and change in identity, as well as the lifelong evolution of attachments and character.

The three main contributions of this book are states of mind observation, person schemas theory, and defensive control processes theory. These three constructs provide a new look at classical topics such as awareness, insight, and developmental change. This leads to the closing chapter on how psychotherapy can enable people to achieve a better integration of character. However, this is not a manual on how to "do" psychotherapy. Instead, the aim is to present in one place the culmination and winnowing of previous work; the new material provides an explicit theoretical basis for understanding change in many contexts.

In the hands of psychotherapists, this approach emphasizes the individuality of each patient and the possibility for case-specific formulations when the guidelines about states of mind, defensive control processes, and person schemas are followed. Systematic methods for using these steps in a configurational analysis is presented in *Formulation as a Basis for Planning Psychotherapy* (Horowitz, 1997b), and technical aspects are presented in *Nuances of Technique in Dynamic Psychotherapy* (Horowitz, 1989c) and *Personality Styles and Brief Psychotherapy* (Horowitz, Marmar, Krupnick, et al., 1984).

An integrated, cognitive-dynamic theory of individual character and emotional relationships can help a person become more aware of his or her own identity. The notion of multiple self schemas, as assembled into larger systems of supraordinate knowledge, addresses this issue directly. Person schemas theory can help one become aware of why connections with others are unsatisfying, why the personal ties they want to preserve are sometimes destroyed. Such understanding leads to insight, decision, and change and can result in an increased sense of self and worth. It enables the individual to form deeper, more mutually satisfying relationships: child–parent attachments, spousal bonds, and cooperative work associations. Efforts in this direction, whether undertaken alone, in psychoeducational practices (as in a relationship with a mentor), or in psychotherapy, can build and integrate character over a lifetime.

Mardi Horowitz
San Francisco

Acknowledgments

I DRAFTED A sketch for this book as a 1983–1984 Fellow at the Center for Advanced Study in the Behavioral Sciences at Stanford under support provided by the John D. and Catherine T. MacArthur Foundation. That foundation then made a dream come true, through an award of two five-year grants, and by appointing me as director of its Program on Conscious and Unconscious Mental Processes. Work with international scientists within that program led to the first draft of this book during a second fellowship year at the Center for Advanced Study in the Behavioral Sciences (1994–1995).

Howard Gardner, Tanya Luhrmann, Kathleen Much, Julia Salzman, Mark Turner, and Jennifer Whiting read the first draft and provided great input. My wife, Carol Ott Horowitz, provided discussion and insight and edited the entire work. Later, readers who amplified ideas and smoothed rough paths included Aubrey Metcalf, Emily Epstein, and Adriana Feder. Carol and Aubrey, my best friends, were best friends of the manuscript.

Colleagues in the Program on Conscious and Unconscious Processes included Susan Anderson, Michel Bond, Gordon Bower, Wilma Bucci, John Conger, Robert Emde, Mathew Erdelyi, Jess Ghannon, Leonard Horowitz, Lester Luborsky, Charles Marmar, Erhart Mergenthaler, Steven Palmer, Christopher Perry, Dana Redington, Howard Shevrin, Zendell Siegal, Jerome Singer, David Spiegel, George Vaillant, Daniel Weiss, Dennise Wolfe, and others.

George Bonanno, Tracy Eells, Mary Ewert, Bram Fridhandler, Andreas Maercker, Constance Milbrath, Steve Reidbord, Charles Stinson, and Hans Znoj are colleagues who helped provide especially valuable empirical foundations to the theory presented.

Virginia Edwards, Gerald Richards, Julia Salzman, and Janet Benjamin well and patiently processed the words. Emily Epstein helped compile the references. Daniel Ott compiled the index and Sandra Gormley produced the printed manuscript, both ably and well. Herb Reich, JoAnn Miller, and everyone at Wiley supported my morale and verve throughout. I thank them all for their excellence and unflagging goodwill.

CHAPTER 1

Conflict

WHEN PEOPLE'S expectations are fulfilled, they feel in equilibrium, they experience harmony of mind. Pleasure and satisfaction flow more abundantly when conflicts do not impair life with antithetical impulses. For many, however, harmony of mind is seldom achieved and when it does occur it is not sustained. Instead, harmony is disrupted by untoward events, discordant ideas, and the eruption of strong but negative emotions such as fear, guilt, shame, hatred, and despair. Impulsive actions may also upset harmony by letting unchecked emotions burst free before consequences are considered, thus causing intended or unintended results. For example, a person hoping for a promotion is challenged by a superior. Instead of cooperating to solve the problem, the person angrily storms out of the office, risking future career advancement, and then later feeling embarrassed.

Experiences of emotional chaos, loss of personal identity, and discord in relationships are often signs of conflict. Such episodes of disharmony occur over both short and long periods. An outburst can occur in a second and a trail of repeated and maladaptive interpersonal behaviors can be found across an entire lifetime.

Opposing forces are a fact of life but need not be intractable. The mind can and does resolve conflicts, sometimes by creating original alternatives. The source of success is not making just one new choice but integrating several new choices with underlying beliefs. This means modifying the structure of those beliefs by changing the association pattern that links them together. This new linkage then forms new attitudes and reduces prior incongruities, mismatches, and discords.

It is difficult to formulate conflict when affection and emotional relationships are involved. The motives, intentions, and even the observable behavioral patterns are multifaceted and layered. Awareness of one facet is incomplete, and just knowing its cause does not lead to optimum decisions resolving a dilemma. For example, a shy man's loneliness conflicts with his desire for closeness. The surface solution would be to learn how to boldly meet new people. However, that conflicts with another trait: he trusts people too much and too soon. He then feels manipulated and abandoned when they are unreliable. His shyness, in part, is defensive. The whole closeness-distance dilemma requires formulation and resolution.

A model for formulating such conflicts has evolved from psychodynamic science. The minimal elements of the model are wishes, fears, and defenses. These elements are in continuous transaction with each other and operate as motives in mental processes. The transactions produce variable end products, such as different states of mind and different states of relating emotionally to others. Whereas many psychoanalytic theories have proven to be untenable, this model has been well supported by evidence and consensual agreement (Horowitz, 1997b; Malan, 1976; Perry, Cooper, & Michels, 1987).

Defenses are key concepts in the psychodynamic model. They prevent unwanted emotional flooding by stifling dangerous urges, and intensify in states when feared consequences of wishes or external situations are anticipated. Some defenses are immediate and short term, as in forgetting about a painful topic for a brief period and then thinking it over in a situation of safety. Other defensive habits are long-term, as in rigid personality traits called "character armor" by Reich (1949). Habitual shyness, as in the man who feared too much closeness, can be such a trait.

Because defensiveness is a part of life, urges to express oneself compete with urges to avoid disclosure to others or with urges to avoid self-acknowledgment. Often, aims to express exist simultaneously with aims to stifle expression (Brenner, 1982; Horowitz, 1988b; Luborsky, 1984; Luborsky & Crits-Cristoph, 1990; Strupp & Binder 1984). Aims to pursue maximum satisfactions are sometimes thwarted by aims to live safely. A balance between such choices is achieved by thought.

Thought is important in reducing conflict or accepting unalterable new situations. Cognitive scientists show how patterns of beliefs are constructed, reconstructed, and generalized (Dennet, 1991; Dixon, 1981; Furster, 1991; Kihlstrom, 1987; Kosslyn & Koenig, 1992; Neisser, 1988). Although cognitive science has focused less on emotional conflict than has psychodynamic science, it has developed a more precise and universal language. This language and theory helps revise prior psychodynamic models such as Freud's libido theory and later structural model of id, ego, and superego (Bucci, 1997; Erdelyi, 1997; Horowitz, 1988b, 1988c, 1991a,b; Singer, 1990; D. Stein, 1997). The resulting integration explains why people find it so difficult to maintain a coherent sense of identity and to correct inappropriate relationship patterns.

Both psychodynamic and cognitive theories include inferences about the mental contents and motivations involved in nonconscious processing. In cognitive science these inferences are most often made about the construction of perceptions and appraisals as based upon biological evidence. But such evidence is still limited when attempting to assess the human brain. More often inferences must be based on careful examination of reports of conscious experience and observation of communication during interpersonal transactions. When the signs of conflict are well described, the mysterious events of unconscious processing can be explained. The following examples of Tim and Marsha illustrate this process.

TIM: INTRUSIVE EMOTION

Tim, a medical student on ward rounds with his surgical resident, entered the room of a patient whom Tim was to examine. As Tim confidently approached the bedside he was startled to feel his pulse suddenly quicken, his stomach knot up, and his muscles tense. This was fear "for no reason"; he thought it made him seem weak. Would his mentor, the resident, or even the patient, think him unfit to be a physician?

At the same moment, Tim was vaguely aware of the odor of a rarely used antiseptic. He had a sense of déja vu, but to fulfill his professional duties he concealed his agitation and competently examined the patient. Later, alone at home, he remembered the smell of that antiseptic and analyzed his anxiety reaction.

As a child, he had throat surgery for a badly infected abscess. He shared a hospital room with a pilot whose face had been extensively burned in a cockpit fire. The pilot's wound became infected, and his condition deteriorated. Tim also developed a complication from his surgery, a postoperative hemorrhage, that awakened him during the night. He felt as if he was suffocating; he noticed there was blood on his pillow. When he coughed up a clot, he became terrified that he was as near to death as the pilot.

Tim had at least two associations that were in conflict. The memory and meanings that formed his positive identity as a young doctor were in conflict with weak and vulnerable feelings he experienced as a child. As Tim entered the hospital room, his interpretations and expectations were organized by the conscious sense of his identity as a capable medical student. He felt safe. An antiseptic smell was consistent with the surroundings. But unconsciously he connected the present, familiar elements to the frightening events in his past and formed a different pattern. Suddenly the room, the patient, the surgeon, and the odor were linked to a traumatic version of himself and it was as if he were again weak, ill, in pain, and afraid for his life. The unconscious association of the odor with this vulnerable identity led to the signs of anxiety. Just when Tim wanted to be a strong and able physician he was thrust back to being a child at great risk.

MARSHA: REPETITIVE INTERPERSONAL RELATIONSHIP PATTERNS

Marsha, a woman in her mid-20s, occasionally and inexplicably acted in ways that were antithetical to her conscious decisions and ability to be assertive, effective, and productive. During the day she was employed as a newspaper journalist and at night worked on a novel. She liked writing her own slant on a story at her job, in accord with her responsible position and excellent skills, but she had a conflict. Sometimes, while preparing an article, instead of proceeding with enthusiasm, she behaved as if she could only function by following explicit instructions from her chief editor. Although he did not welcome this timidity, he would tell her how to do the piece if she seemed indecisive. Marsha did not intend to be passive, and at these times tried to counteract any submissive stance. Where, she wondered, was her usual confidence?

Marsha also noted a conflicting cycle in her pattern of intimate associations with men. Every time she entered into a relationship, seeking closeness, the relationship would quickly sour. She would blame the man for taking over her identity and for becoming emotionally distant. Then she would feel trapped and break off the connection.

Joe, her domestic partner at the time, wrote technical manuals for a corporation but really wanted to write and publish novels. Marsha had already succeeded in publishing small sections of her intended novel as short stories or as works in progress. She wanted Joe to be pleased with her accomplishment as an author, but she knew he felt bitter about his lack of achievement. She noted his envy of writers who were getting their stories published and thought Joe might become jealous of her success. As a result she lied to him about her work, saying she had stopped writing her novel.

Marsha was baffled by her behavior. It impaired her chances for success and satisfaction at her job, at home, and in her creative enterprises. When thinking about her behavior at work, she was aware that her chief did not tell her what to do unless she acted too passively when presenting her story line. He was not threatened by her doing well and, in fact, praised her in a generous way. Yet in some states of mind Marsha submissively invited his instructions even though she had conscious intentions to act otherwise. She was aware she had this submissive pattern but had little insight into why she repeated it.

When Marsha considered her relationship with Joe, she saw a similar pattern, although there seemed to be more reason for her submissiveness with him than with her editor. Joe, unlike her editor, might feel diminished in their intimate relationship because of her greater competence and productivity. In her past relationships, she noted the same pattern, and so she began to wonder: Did she pick men who would feel threatened and inferior to her? Did she compromise too often, looking to them for reflections of her identity? Marsha wondered why this cycle kept recurring against her clearest conscious wishes.

In psychotherapy Marsha became aware of her irrational belief that all men would feel envious and hurt by her superior achievements. She also saw she avoided being productive to prevent their anticipated hurt and envy. With this insight, she was then able to increase her productivity by planning and practicing how to present her creative work frankly, amiably, and competently to men, rather than being excessively forward or too fearful. When she was able to do this, she found men more supportive than she expected.

Through the therapeutic process of awareness, insight, and new decisions, Marsha was able to cease repetition of her unproductive cycles. She had a good level of awareness about her behavior patterns that conflicted with her conscious intentions, but she needed more information to explain how and why she repeated these self-impairing patterns. Therapy helped her gain insight into the cycles of her states of mind and the causes for making transitions from one state to another.

AWARENESS, INSIGHT, DECISION

Tim, the medical student, had signs of conflict that included unwelcome intrusions of awareness with a secondary fear of losing control. Recognizing these signs of conflict, he went through a sequence of awareness and insight. He recognized what was happening as he reviewed the events in his childhood memory. He increased awareness by arriving at a label for his state of mind in the hospital room: fear. He developed insight by understanding the probable reasons for his adult transition into a state of fear. He linked the shift in his state of mind to the smell of the unusual antiseptic, and then he connected this smell to a past traumatic experience.

Tim used this insight in an obvious way. He made a decision to prepare himself by being alert for this smell in the future. Thus he would prevent a startle or alarm reaction, just as a runner at the starting block is prepared for a gunshot and bursts forward rather than jumping skyward.

In the second example, Marsha had defensive reasons for avoiding assertive action. The operation of these defenses were obscure to her before therapy, she did not understand why she behaved as she did. In therapy she increased her recognition. First, she heightened her awareness of her transitions into states of unassertive activity. Then she developed insight into why this occurred by recognizing that a contradiction existed between her intentions and her actions, she was afraid of being more successful than men and feared the negative consequences would strain her relationships.

She decided to give more attention to her conflicts and to certain ideas and feelings. By anticipating her expectations in her transactions with men, she was able to curb her passive or timid behavior.

She rehearsed her new choice, which was to use her skill fully, even when she dreaded hurting another person's feelings. She learned that the feared consequences happened only rarely, if at all. She decided to alter her expectations in a careful, repeated, conscious rehearsal of what was likely and what was unlikely to happen.

Marsha changed through a sequence of interacting mental and social activities. This sequence began with her self-observations, and each change she made increased her observational skills and also her other capacities. Figure 1.1 provides a generalization of this psychological pattern of change.

Tim and Marsha illustrate a sequence of awareness, insight, and new decisions. This happens at three major levels: states of mind, altering defensive controls of ideas and emotions, and person schemas. This organizational scaffold is shown in Table 1.1

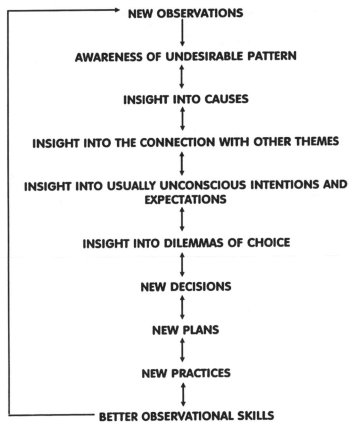

FIGURE 1.1
AWARENESS, INSIGHT, AND NEW DECISIONS

TABLE 1.1
STATES, CONTROLS, AND PERSON SCHEMAS IN RELATION TO
AWARENESS, INSIGHT, AND DECISION

	Awareness	Insight	Decision
States	Knowing when a change occurs	Understanding how and why a change occurs	Planning how to avoid repeating maladaptive state cycles
Altering Controls	Recognizing avoidance of a conflicted topic	Realizing how and why the defensiveness occurs	Choosing to focus attention on a usually warded-off topic
Person Schemas	Knowing preconscious concepts of self and others	Anticipating how and why intentions and actions may shift	Choosing and rehearsing new roles to avoid repeating a maladaptive pattern

SUMMARY

A sense of coherence or even harmony can be restored by making new decisions to change elements in a conflict. Integration can also be achieved by establishing a larger belief system that connects meanings and synthesizes the competing elements operating in smaller belief systems. Conscious insight can foster such new decisions and help form reconciling schemas. Unconscious mental computations also work to revise information. When problems are difficult to solve and dilemmas impede any solution, conscious awareness is especially important.

Even though conscious thought is highly useful for solving difficult problems, conflict can lead to both heightened impulsivity and heightened defensiveness. Conscious thought itself may be blocked. Only the emergent signs of conflict reveal the dynamic tensions between various nonconscious intentions and expectations. Observing such signs—and the differences among desired, dreaded, and defensive states of mind—leads to an understanding of emotional problems; this is the starting point for finding solutions.

CHAPTER 2

States of Mind

I N DIFFERENT states of mind people contemplate the same topic of conflict in various ways: for example, a person who decides to stay in an ambivalent relationship in one state might decide to end it in another. Observing differences in attitude in various states can clarify the nature of the conflict.

In some states of mind, the difficult topic is ignored or touched on with numb emotions. In other states, waves of uncontrollable feeling flood the person whenever a reminder of the topic occurs. Sometimes both displays of emotion and efforts to stifle feelings to occur simultaneously. And at other times, even with unpleasant emotion, the person thinks and feels deeply about the difficult topic without sensing any lapse in control. This chapter covers this range of experience of self-regulation. It also covers the range of states of mind: between desire and dread, between wished-for states of emotion, and those that people fear most.

Attention to states of mind and their labeling can lead to heightened awareness and clarification. Recognizing patterns and shifts in states and analyzing the cycles of states often illuminates motivation and clears the way for the understanding of conflict and its possible resolution.

DEFINING STATES OF MIND

A *state of mind* is a combination of conscious and unconscious experiences with patterns of behavior that can last for a short or long period of time (Allen, 1977; Carr, 1983; Doherty, Von Kanmer, Siros, & Marder, 1978; Federn, 1952; Gaarter, 1971; Horowitz, 1979b, 1987). Each person has a repertoire of recurrent states of mind. Sometimes, when asked, he or she can describe the state experienced at the time, at least partially. In addition, observers can learn, often unconsciously, to recognize the states of mind of another person with whom they become familiar.

Good observers, such as psychotherapists, raise these recognitions to clear statements about the pattern of qualities. These descriptions usually involve some combination of styles of bodily posture, gesture and movement, emotional qualities of relating self to others, and ways of thinking about and coping with danger. A state involves a wide range of features, but the most important include these three: emotionality, control of emotionality, and desires or fears about emotional relationships.

States of mind are perceived differently depending on whether one observes another or contemplates oneself introspectively. The self may have some ideas and feelings that are kept concealed from willful disclosure. Yet in frank communications, when the self and the observer agree, their awareness becomes more acute because they can recognize repertoires of personal states. Both parties can note certain verbal and nonverbal expressions, as well as specific patterns for describing the self and others in various states. Only the self can know inner identity experiences, and a sense of being part of a relationship, but communication and empathic recognition can include the observing other.

A familiar example of the salience of a state of mind is when people greet each other by saying, "How are you?" and responding, "I am fine" (or "I am not well"). Beyond this ritual courtesy, such an exchange between friends is based on the utility of signaling a current state of well- or ill-being. One translation of these ritual remarks: "Are you in your usual state? Can we go on where we left off?" "Yes, I am as you expect, let us continue," or "No, my state has changed, be aware I am now in distress, angry, and lacking in self-control."

States of mind index inner emotion and degree of control over urgent feelings. The degrees of control range from excessive stifling to impulsive expression. When someone is angry, he may tell a companion he is dangerous because his state is one of loss of control over hostility, or he may tell a companion he is well modulated and ready for conversation that may resolve frustrations. Sometimes he may manifest a stone face, a seeming calm that is emotionally rigid, telling a sagacious companion to be careful lest hostile intentions lurk beneath the mask.

LABELING STATES

Labeling states of mind falls into three main categories. The first portrays the emotional coloration of a mood, such as *depressed* or *anxious*. These are general labels that are given to describe primary emotions. Idiosyncratic labels such as *tensely vigilant* or *morose blues* can be used to heighten personal awareness and describe individualized states. The second main category describes state regulation using the terms undermodulated, overmodulated, well-modulated, and shimmering. These themes are examined next. The third category labels states by type of motivation, such as wished for or dreaded states. It also includes those quasi-adaptive and problematic states that people defensively use to avoid entry into states they dread. This third category is described in the section "Type of Motivation found on page 22." All three categories are illustrated in Table 2.1.

DEGREE OF EMOTIONAL REGULATION

In day-to-day life most people operate in a well-modulated range. Of course, styles of expression vary among cultures—some are more expressive, some more reserved—but when a person is operating outside the middle range it will be noticeable. What is described here holds for industrialized Western culture, but both under- and overmodulated states commonly occur after traumatic life events in all societies.

Undermodulated states include impulsive actions and unregulated displays of ideas and feelings. Expressions of emotion can seem explosive, blatant, or raw. Pangs of usually restrained feeling erupt and can lead to unwelcome action. Fear and anxiety are often added to the experience because of a sense of losing control: fear can become panic, rage can become abuse, and self-disgust can lead to suicidal impulses. Many psychiatric symptoms occur frequently in undermodulated states.

During *overmodulated states*, people appear excessively self-restrained or rigid. They maintain a poker face, pretend unfelt attitudes, or manifest indifference to friendly empathy. An inability to

TABLE 2.1
STATE CATEGORIZATIONS
(EXAMPLES OF GENERAL AND IDIOSYNCRATIC LABELS)

Categorically Emphasized Feature	General	Idiosyncratic
Emotion	Anxious	Tensely vigilant
	Depressed	Morose blues
Regulation of Emotion	Well modulated	Assertive confrontation
	Undermodulated	Blurted-out rage
	Overmodulated	Stonily ironic
	Shimmering	Timorous whining
Motivation	Desired (usually well modulated)	Joyous intimacy
	Dreaded (often under-modulated)	Violently destructive
	Problematic compromise (frequently shimmering)	Anxiously suspicious
	Quasi-adaptive compromise (sometimes overmodulated)	Cool and aloof

shift out of an overmodulated state into a spontaneous, intimate, en-gaged state impairs one's ability to love and work well and explains many rigid aspects of personality, such as *traits* of woodenness with lack of passion or creative sparkle.

In *well-modulated states*, a relatively harmonious accord across modes of expression is observed. The person feels and appears to be in self-control, even when expressing intense and distressing emo-tions and troublesome ideas.

Shimmering states combine features of the three other states. They have an oscillating and discordant pattern of elements. Leakage of emotional expression alternates rapidly with efforts to suppress it. Conflicting emotions rise to awareness. A feeling expressed in a facial movement may discord with an emotion conveyed in words, vocal tone, blushing, or body movements. A person in a shimmering state may experience and express antithetical views about what is happening in a relationship, as in moving both closer and becoming more distant, being both interested and suspicious, or being both approachable and avoidant. One notices the quick shuffling of contradictory expressions, verbal and nonverbal.

These four categories of states, as differentiated by apparent and relative control of emotion, are summarized in Table 2.2. Using these general state categories, judges can reliably rate videotapes of people involved in the discourse of psychotherapy. During shimmering and undermodulated states, topics related to current and unresolved emotional conflicts occurred significantly more frequently (Horowitz, Milbrath, Jordan, et al., 1994; Horowitz, Milbrath & Ewert, et al., 1994; Horowitz, Ewert, Milbrath, 1996). In overmodulated states, these conflicted topics were discussed rarely or only superficially.

Consider the various states of fear. An undermodulated state would involve uncontrolled panic. A well-modulated expression of fear can be frank and direct. During a shimmering state, the individual may be striving to appear calm while conspicuously leaking signs of fear by furtive eye movements, halting speech, and sweaty palms. This state is common during public speeches and performances by people who do not frequently engage in those activities.

Overmodulated states can serve as a defense against a dreaded transition into anticipated, undermodulated states. For example, some schizophrenic patients know they have an unwanted, involuntary tendency to enter into undermodulated states that are characterized by intrusive hallucinations and irrational but impulsive actions based on delusional beliefs. Very often such patients try to prevent transition into such states by utilizing an overmodulated state characterized by irony, mockery, sarcasm, and facetiousness. They rigidly control impulses and show instead a heightened display of decorum that can reach the point of absurdity. They might hesitantly act, interrupt the action, and then act very slowly, only to interrupt it again (Sass, 1992).

TABLE 2.2
CONTROL OF EMOTION:
GENERAL DEFINITIONS OF SOME STATES OF MIND

Undermodulated States	Undermodulated states appear to the observer as if the individual has dysregulation of emotional expression. This leads to appraisals of the individual as impulsive, uncontrolled, or experiencing intrusive concepts and emotions. Sharp increases in the intensity of expressions may suddenly appear as the individual experiences flares, surges, or pangs of emotion. The observer may experience surges of emotion as an empathic response, or perhaps feel a wish to intervene in a way that will help the patient regain control.
Well-Modulated States	Well-modulated states exemplify a relatively smooth flow of expressions. Affective displays appear genuine, and regardless of intensity, are expressed in a poised manner. The observer may feel subjective interest and empathy, with a sense of being connected to the individual and the material presented. The observer appraises the individual as engaged in an organized process of communication without major discords between verbal and nonverbal modes of expression.
Overmodulated States	Overmodulated states are characterized by excessive control of expressive behavior. The individual seems stiff, enclosed, masked, or walled-off. To the observer, the individual's emotional displays—if present—may seem feigned or false. The observer appraises the individual as distant from genuine communication. Therefore, the observer may feel disconnected from the individual, even bored or inattentive.
Shimmering States	Shimmering states are characterized by the individual shifting rapidly between undercontrolled emotions and overcontrolled emotion. The observer may recognize discordant signs of expression in verbal and nonverbal modes. The clashing signals may occur simultaneously or within a brief period of time.

THE EFFECTS OF STRESS

Stress (for example, a time pressure to reach a decision or act) increases emotional conflict by raising one's awareness of danger. Even when external stressor life events appear to be over in the social context, they continue to work as stressors in the psychological and bio-logical contexts of the person. Stress is completed only when physical and mental equilibrium is restored. Until such completion is reached, stress causes a deflection from ordinary states of mind (Janis, 1969).

In particular, opposite deflections occur; for example after a trauma, a person might have more undermodulated states and also more overmodulated states. As he or she works on the memory of the event, the person might have frequent shimmering states. Well modulated, ordinary states are restored when a point of relative completion has been reached.

After experiencing very stressful life events, such as those involving natural disasters, a person might find that unpleasant memories and fantasies intrude as unwanted images during undermodulated states. Paradoxically, in overmodulated states, omissive experiences also increase, and memories can even be lost for a time, as in repressed memory phenomena. The self unconsciously tries to avoid emotional flooding and the sense of feeling out of control.

My colleagues and I studied people after stressful life events. Some subjects had been given sudden bad news about risk factors for future illnesses when they believed they were in a state of good health and had no symptoms (Horowitz, et al., 1980). Other subjects were volunteers who underwent vicarious stressor events through the use of films and videotapes shown in our laboratory setting (Horowitz & Becker, 1972a,b; Horowitz, 1975b; Horowitz, 1997). Additional subjects interviewed had experienced real frights, injuries, or losses. We found that all three groups reported increased rates of intrusive and omissive experiences and of related under- and overmodulated states. Signs or symptoms of intrusion and omission came to be recognized as cardinal phenomena in establishing diagnostic criteria for posttraumatic stress disorder (American Psychiatric Association, 1980; Horowitz, 1977b; Horowitz, Wilner, Kaltreider, & Alvarez, 1980).

Undermodulated states contained increased levels and frequency of expression of unwanted ideas, unbidden images, memory (and fantasy) repetitions, and pangs of feelings related to the stressor event. Overmodulated states contained avoidance, denial, disavowal, and emotional numbing. Phases of response were noted in which many people oscillated in defensiveness, leading to sequences of under- and overmodulated states. (Horowitz 1972a, 1973, 1977b;

Horowitz, Wilner, & Alvarez, 1979; Horowitz, Wilner, et al., 1980). These phases are illustrated in Figures 2.1 and 2.2.

The first phase, emotional *outcry*, includes piercing feelings and racing thoughts. The person might have an alarm reaction and feel revolted by thoughts such as "I can never get over this!" or "This must be my fault!" An overmodulated phase of *denial* might follow: Emotional regulation is sharply increased, feelings are dampened, and a sense of numbing occurs. The stressed person can, for a while, experience only a dim memory of the traumatic incident or deny certain personal implications. Key topics and potential emotional responses are sometimes omitted from conscious thought. During these states, some people experience a sense of strange identity, depersonalization, or dissociation.

A phase of *sharp emotional experiences*, or *intrusions*, such as flashbacks, memories, fantasies, could then occur. If so, the person can shift into an undermodulated state. This phase sometimes replicates the outcry phase but tends to exist for a longer period. Reminders of fright and loss trigger more intense startle reactions and somatic alarms.

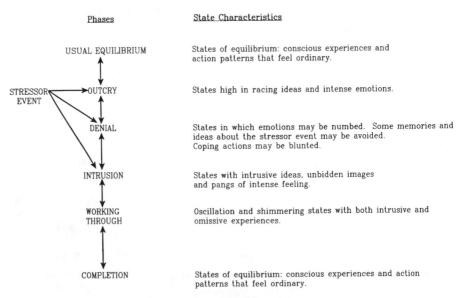

FIGURE 2.1
PHASES OF RESPONSE AFTER STRESSFUL LIFE EVENTS

Phases   Pathologic States

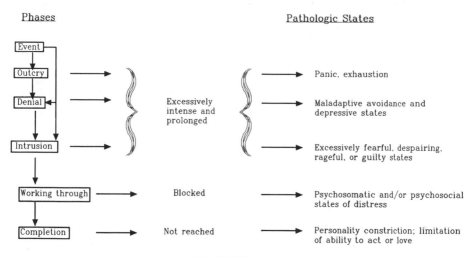

FIGURE 2.2

STATES PRECIPITATED BY STRESSOR EVENTS

Over time, people realize that the memories and fantasies about the event are understandable and that new schematizations of identity are developing. Shimmering states tend to replace under- or overmodulated states. This is the *working through* phase.

At this point, the trauma is contemplated with relatively controlled but still distressing emotional expressions. During phases of working through, the person often oscillates, or shimmers between numbness and pangs of feeling, between intrusive and avoidant thoughts about the event, between recognizing and avoiding its implications. Gradually, emotional turbulence resolves as the meaning of the stressor event is integrated with beliefs about the past and expectations for the future. Pangs of feeling and intrusive ideas subside and a state of *completion* is achieved.

Not everyone follows this sequence. Some people go directly into states of defensive withdrawal from the emotional implications of a stressor event. Others respond with states in which intrusive ideas and emotions make them feel out of control. Yet others have a resilient response and adapt well to adversity; they cope rapidly, experiencing only a brief emotional perturbation. Individual responses vary from resilient to normal and pathological stress, as outlined in Table 2.3 and Figure 2.2.

TABLE 2.3
DIFFERENT PHASES OF RESPONSE TO STRESSOR EVENTS

Time	Resilient Response	Normal Stress Response	Pathological Stress Response
Before event	Equilibrium (well-modulated states)	Equilibrium (well-modulated states)	Equilibrium (or pre-event turbulence)
During event	Emotional perturbation	Outcry	Prolonged undermodulated states
After event	Equilibrium	Denial	Excessive and prolonged overmodulated states
		Intrusion	Excessive and prolonged undermodulated and overmodulated states
		Working through with return to well-modulated states	Failure to adapt to new circumstances and to achieve well-modulated states
		Completion with Equilibrium	Reschematization of identity into a pathological equilibrium

Table 2.4 outlines co-occurring signs during a denial phase of response to stress. Table 2.5 does the same for an intrusive phase (Horowitz, 1992; Horowitz, Wilner, Kaltreider, et al., 1980; McFarlane, Norman, Streiner, & Roy 1984; Zilberg, Weiss, & Horowitz, 1982).

TYPE OF MOTIVATION

In the discussion of labeling states, the issue of general categories of states according to motivational dimensions was touched upon. Such categories include *desired states*, *dreaded states*, and *states utilized defensively*. These defensive compromises help people avoid entry into dreaded states of mind. Through research, they have been found to be usefully divided into those that are *problematic*, as when anxiety occurs, and those that are without such symptoms but still only achieve a *quasi-adaptive* rather than fully adaptive stance.

A configuration of states places them into a diagram with quad-

TABLE 2.4
COMMON CO-OCCURRENCES DURING A DENIAL PHASE
OF RESPONSE TO STRESS

Awareness and focus of attention	Selective inattention leading to inability to appreciate significance of some facts.
	Avoidance of certain stress related topics.
Processing of ideas	Minimization of meanings to the self by substitutions, inhibitions, disavowals, or misinformation.
	Rapid conclusion of conflictual topics.
	Fantasies to counteract reality.
Emotional manifestations	Numbness.
Somatic manifestations	Bodily preoccupations, aches, tensions, bowel disturbances, sleep disturbances.
Actions	Absence of satisfaction with usually meaningful activities.
	Self-isolation from reminders.

rants for *desired state, dreaded state, problematic compromise*, and *quasi-adaptive compromise*. In the midst of high stress after a serious life event, and before all its meanings to the self have been assimilated, a person yearns for the restoration of a prior equilibrium: a desired state. Memories and fantasies about the dire event cause the person to fear entry into the pit of intense and uncontrolled emotional flooding: a dreaded state. The person might have anxiety even during a dose-by-dose recollection and contemplation of implications of the event: a problematic compromise state. The person might avoid recollection and work on the meanings of the stressor topics, therefore having a semblance of emotional equilibrium: This solution is only

TABLE 2.5
COMMON CO-OCCURRENCES DURING AN INTRUSION PHASE
OF RESPONSE TO STRESS

Awareness and focus of attention	Hypervigilance.
	Startle reactions.
	Intrusive-repetitive thoughts, unbidden images, nightmares or bad dreams.
Processing of ideas	Overgeneralization of other topics to stress related topics leading to preoccupation and inability to concentrate on other topics.
Emotional manifestations	Emotional attacks as sharp "pangs."
	Pining and yearning.
Somatic manifestations	Exhaustion from chronic "fight or flight" readiness.
	Bowel and muscle symptoms
	Sleep disturbances.
Actions	Compulsive repetitions of events or pointless searches for lost persons and situations.

quasi-adaptive because assimilation could be blocked by this defensive stance.

Such a configuration after a generic stressor event is shown in Figure 2.3. The desired state is, in terms already discussed, usually well modulated; the dreaded state could be labeled as undermodulated; and the problematic state might be called a shimmering state. The motivational terms such as desired and dreaded or compromise states indicate psychodynamics: the configuration of wish, fear, and defense that occurs within an emotionally conflicted mind. The self-regulatory terms such as under and overmodulated indicate the

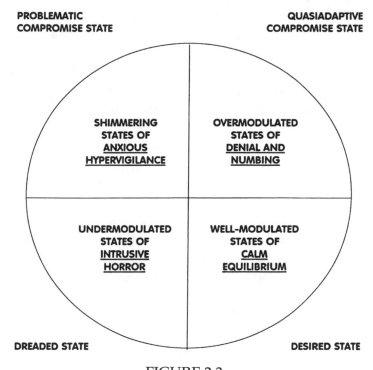

PROBLEMATIC
COMPROMISE STATE

QUASIADAPTIVE
COMPROMISE STATE

SHIMMERING
STATES OF
ANXIOUS
HYPERVIGILANCE

OVERMODULATED
STATES OF
DENIAL AND
NUMBING

UNDERMODULATED
STATES OF
INTRUSIVE
HORROR

WELL-MODULATED
STATES OF
CALM
EQUILIBRIUM

DREADED STATE

DESIRED STATE

FIGURE 2.3

A CONFIGURATION OF STATES AFTER A TRAUMATIC LIFE EVENT

sense or appearance of efforts to control expressions. In observation, the latter are usually clarified first. Then motivational configurations can be inferred.

It's "manly" to be undermodulated

STATE TRANSITIONS AND STATE CYCLES

Stressor events challenge adaptation and disturb equilibrium. They often trigger a transition from a well-modulated state into one that is under- or overmodulated. Imagine someone in a hospital waiting room who has just received very bad news from a doctor, saying loudly and with a grimace, "I don't think I can take it" and then louder, with sobs, "I just *can't take it*!" Another person in the same situation might respond to the bad news differently, shifting from a concerned but normal expressiveness to a stony face and say flatly, "So that's that." The first example is a shift from a well-modulated into an undermodulated state; the second is a shift from a well-modulated state into an overmodulated state.

Stressor events provide striking examples, but state change patterns are often quite important to observe in less dramatic circumstances. Most especially, transactional problems in relationships can be clarified by observing cyclic state transition patterns. The following story illustrates such repetitive shifts. A theme of anger and social bitterness runs across this cycle of states.

Jim

Jim, an intelligent, 40-year-old business executive, had been successful in situations in which he worked on his own within his corporation. Jim knew of his tendency to hot-tempered states, so he usually kept to himself. He had been rewarded with a promotion for his creative approach to marketing the company's products. Following his promotion, Jim took on supervisory responsibilities and had to present the work from his unit to a management committee.

This recent success imposed more stress on Jim's weakest area of functioning, his relationships with others. When people he supervised did not meet his expectations, Jim sometimes exploded into a rage; afterward, he shifted into a withdrawn, uncommunicative state. Both his rages and his withdrawal threatened his career future; he had been warned but found that he could not change his behavior. He had an increased frequency of tense and jittery states in anticipation of being fired. At this point, he complained about his anxiety to his physician. After a three-month period of drug treatment for an anxiety disorder characterized by social phobia and tension, he was referred for individual psychotherapy. The anti-anxiety medication had only partially relieved his symptoms and supportive advice from the physician had not counteracted his social withdrawal.

During his subsequent treatment, Jim spoke ambiguously about being upset with others and offered no further clarification of his hostility. The therapist was quiet until the pattern was noted; then he focused on this important theme. The first step was to clarify how episodes of anger led to problems and what happened before, during, and after these episodes. When Jim agreed with the importance of this focal topic, the second step was to understand various states in which anger was or was not experienced. Jim and his therapist worked out a list of states in which his anger appeared. They ranged in degree of control from undermodulated to overmodulated, as shown in Table 2.6.

TABLE 2.6
JIM'S ANGRY STATES

General Label	Individualized Label
Undermodulated	Blind rage
Well-modulated	Annoyance; Bantering sarcasm
Overmodulated	Stony, sullen, and grudging
Shimmering	Blurting out with stifling

Jim's undermodulated state was labeled *blind rage*.[1] In this frame of mind, Jim had impulses to devastate any frustrating person; at those moments, he was not aware that he had ever even liked the person. Instead, he exaggerated their faults and irrationally blamed them.

Jim had a less eruptive but shimmering state in which he sometimes *blurted out irritation* but also tried to *stifle* his expressions of anger. Jim also expressed anger in two well-modulated states called *annoyance* and *bantering sarcasm*. In the state of *annoyance*, he monitored his anger and how he was expressing it to others. He felt his sharpness was appropriate and fully under his control. While expressing his annoyance, he did not exaggerate the blame. During the *bantering sarcasm* state, Jim handled feelings of hostility by teasing others in a good-tempered and genuinely humorous way, and at the same time he could tolerate receiving witty barbs from others.

Jim also had an overmodulated state for expressing hostility: He was *stony*, *sullen*, and *grudging*. He was aware of his potential for anger and did not want to show this to others. Within himself he felt that he was a solid rock and impervious to irritation. On closer self-examination and insight, however, Jim realized that his stony demeanor and aloofness were actually experienced as hostility by some of his peers. His suppression of feelings caused him to speak very

---

[1]As mentioned previously, general labels for states can follow emotions (depressed, anxious, angry), regulation (under-, over-, and well-modulated), and motivation (desired, dreaded, defensive compromises). In self-developmental observations and during psychotherapy, it is best to be less general after initial observations and more specific to the individual. This leads to idiosyncratic labels. As a convention, for clarity, in this text these idiosyncratic labels will always be in italics.

carefully, with precise wording. He did not react spontaneously to others but instead crept slowly through an interchange, making the other individual uncomfortable by his lack of spontaneity.

Jim revealed a fantasy of what he expected from his treatment. He desired to have no further experiences of rage, to have the therapist remove this emotion from contaminating his life. When this expectation was communicated, it became clear to Jim, on reflection, that it was not within the range of human possibility to be expunged of all rage. Nonetheless, he was angry with the therapist and expected him to feel terribly ashamed that he could not produce what his patient wanted.

Jim's expectation that the therapist would feel an extreme and searing state of *shame* soon led to an examination of Jim's own potential for entry into a dreaded state of *shameful mortification*. Gradually, he revealed a tendency to experience himself in the role of a ridiculously weak pretender who could suddenly be exposed for imposture and incompetence. He attempted to avoid any entry into the dreaded and undermodulated state of *shameful mortification* because he anticipated that it would be disastrous to his sense of identity.

Configurations of States: Inferring Motivational Patterns

Pragmatically, one can consider Jim's wishes as *desired* states of mind and his related fears as *dreaded* ones. People unconsciously calculate, as well as sometimes consciously anticipate, future possible states. These levels of expectation often include *wish–fear dilemmas*. A wish–fear dilemma consists of goals that involve actions that could satisfy desires but could also lead to threatening situations. To defend against the danger of dreaded states, defensive control processes can form *compromise states*.

Compromise states are neither what is most desired nor what is most dreaded. They can blunt emotion and seem almost adaptive, or they can contain emotions that defend against what one fears most intensely. For example, a person might dread a state of guilt for harming someone. This state is avoided by becoming angry at the other (on the premise that you need not feel guilty over someone who has irked you). The compromise, because it is itself distressing, can be called a *problematic state*. A person might seek out help because of experiences in problematic compromise states and then discover that there are even worse states, ones even more dreaded.

Jim was asked what states he desired. His prominent and repeated stories indicated that he hoped for periods of success with *joyous* and *exhibitionistic excitement*. By showing his work to others, he imagined he would gain their admiration and feel pride. But, in reality, showing his work to others could lead into either this desired state of *exhibitionistic excitement* or to an automatically associated state of dreaded *shameful mortification*. Showing his work was associated with a wish–fear dilemma: He anticipated that it would lead to either a highly desired or a highly dreaded state. If he did not present his work, he avoided *shameful mortification* but reduced his chances of *exhibitionistic excitement*. Instead of either the desired or the dreaded state, he withdrew from contact and, alone in his office, often entered a state of *ruminative rehearsal*. This state avoided conscious fantasies of either great humiliation or great success and had an unsatisfying—but calming—effect.

The *ruminative rehearsal* state did not have negative emotions and so it was a *quasi-adaptive compromise*. Within it, Jim felt reasonably comfortable, but he could not achieve the pleasurable excitement he desired; so this state was not fully adaptive. He just rehearsed in a nonprogressive way, without ever concluding that he was ready to show good work to others.

When Jim was required to present his ideas or meet with his team, this compromise state of *isolated, ruminative rehearsal* was not adaptive. He became *anxiously worried* or blamed others and expressed *blind rage*. But both processes were problematic compromises and, as such, unsatisfying. The configuration of states Jim desired, dreaded, or used as defensive compromises can serve as an abstract model of his motivation, as sketched in Figure 2.4.

Maladaptive interpersonal behavioral patterns often include a relatively inflexible sequence of shifts in states, a cycle that repeats itself. Cycles might have variations, but a generalized pattern can be formulated. When he showed work, Jim would begin with the desired state of *exhibitionistic excitement* but then tended to shift from the wish to receive admiring attention to anticipation of a dreaded state of *shameful mortification*. To avoid the distress of this state, he shifted into *anxious worry*. He would quickly shift from worry to rage as he found a subordinate to blame for a weak or bad performance. Finally, to restore equilibrium, he would withdraw into a state of *ruminative rehearsal*. Eventually, the wish to show his work, or social pressure, led him to anticipate *exhibitionistic excitement*, which is

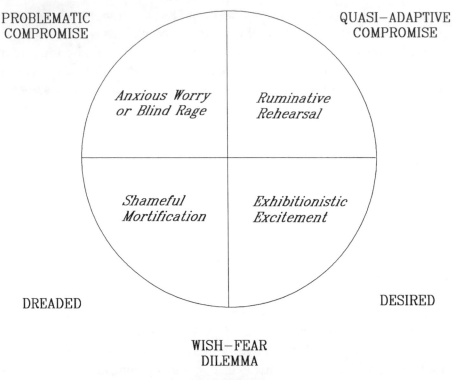

PROBLEMATIC
COMPROMISE

QUASI–ADAPTIVE
COMPROMISE

Anxious Worry
or Blind Rage

Ruminative
Rehearsal

Shameful
Mortification

Exhibitionistic
Excitement

DREADED

DESIRED

WISH–FEAR
DILEMMA

FIGURE 2.4
A MOTIVATIONAL CONFIGURATION OF JIM'S STATES

where this cycle started and the repetition of it recurs, as shown in Figure 2.5.

Some aspects of a state cycle are hidden from observers and more commonly from the self. Jim and his work partners were familiar with his defensive compromise states of *rage, worry,* and *rumination.* The deeper motivational states of desiring *excited self exhibition* and dreading *shame* were relatively concealed from others and only vaguely available to Jim's own conscious reflections. He shifted his attention away from thinking about wishes and fears, leaving his awareness in a cloudy, unclear zone.

SUMMARY

Any type of emotion can be experienced in different ways in various states of mind. One can experience sadness in a *distraught sobbing* state, in a *poignant* but *resigned melancholy,* or the *rigid smiling* state of

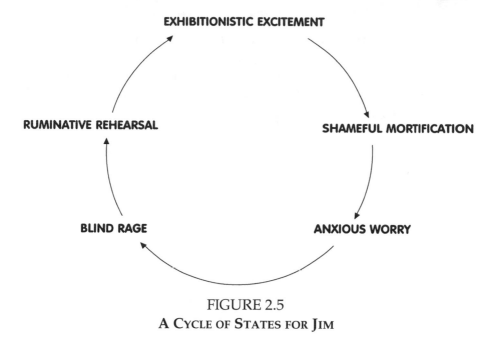

FIGURE 2.5
A CYCLE OF STATES FOR JIM

masked despair. One state of mind differs from another, not only in types of emotion, but also in types of blended feelings and degree of control. Personal identity is experienced differently in different states. Qualities of emotional transaction in an ongoing relationship also vary from state to state, as domestic partners well know about each other.

Labeling states increases understanding of how one comes to feel the way one does. Undermodulated, overmodulated, well-modulated, and shimmering states indicate the degree of emotional regulation. Well-modulated states are those in which a person is in self-command: appropriately spontaneous, openly expressive, harmonious in verbal and nonverbal communications, and controlled in acting on, or containing impulses. Undermodulated states are those in which expressions are excessively impulsive. Overmodulated states are those in which the person is excessively veiled or pretending to a role. Shimmering states have discordant features of emotions and controls.

Other labels can be used to indicate motivation: dreaded states are feared, desired states are wished for, and compromise states are used to achieve defensive aims. People who gain awareness of their state shifts and develop insight into why they experience unwanted states can alter their current patterns and often learn how to shift into more desired ones. They can develop a heightened awareness of the cues that bring about desired states and the triggers that provoke dreaded states. With this knowledge, preparations can be made to maximize desired states and avoid the repetition of maladaptive cycles.

CHAPTER 3

Awareness

Unbonded - no insight/awareness

AWARENESS VARIES in different states of mind. Upon reflection many people recognize what state of mind they are in and compare it with other states. They become aware of how their present identity experience differs from other experiences of self and, with effort, they gain insight into why such variations occur. They can contemplate painful topics and previously unresolved conflicts. They can rework previously avoided memories and fantasies. Awareness and insight then lead to new decisions that promote changes in self concepts and plans. As a result, doors open to new possibilities and behaviors.

Reflective awareness is important because it can help one compare beliefs and replay memories. Each repetition may add alternative interpretations of meaning; one repetition could give a "blue" interpretation, another a "yellow" one. Eventually, contemplation rearranges beliefs and one can reach optimal "green" solutions to various problems.

Through examination of different linkages between associated ideas, people can decipher cause-and-effect sequences. For example, when a person hears the words, *Jack and Jill,* he or she might immediately think of the words *went up the hill.* The person has heard so many times the story about how Jack and Jill fetched a pail of water that he strongly associates one set of words with the other. Insight is seeing the repeated pattern and, as in this instance, knowing that the sequence comes to mind because of prior repetitions. Awareness of the outside input of *Jack and Jill,* and the inner addition of *went up the hill* all lead to such insight.

Insight expands with every recognition of how one pattern connects to another. With insight, the person can make new decisions. The resulting choices change the matrix of associated meanings; some associational linkages are made stronger, others weaker. With new choices come modifications in expectations, goals, and priorities.

The sequence of awareness, insight, and choice can combine a sense of an *experiencing self* with a sense of an *observing self.* Change processes based on insight occur more readily in the minds of people who have, or can develop, this combined *observing–experiencing* form of contemplation. But change also occurs at many other levels of awareness, and it is desirable to have a set of categories and a model for describing where the mind processes information.

After careful review of contemporary research, Farthing (1992) provided the triangular model of levels of information processing shown in Figure 3.1.

The apex of the triangle in Figure 3.1 contains *reflective consciousness,* where self-awareness and introspection take place. Below it are other levels of awareness. One of these is *primary consciousness:* It includes an awareness of ideas, feelings, and perceptions without the complexity of the observing self reflecting on the experiencing self. Another mode of awareness, called *peripheral awareness,* includes recognition of stimuli that are only vaguely known. These peripherally registered stimuli are stored in consciously retrievable short-term memory and can later become a focus of attention in primary consciousness. Below that, at the base of the triangle, are sectors of nonconscious knowledge. These sources of know-how lead to the unconscious computing power of the mind, which can process more information than can be consciously represented at one time.

In this model, a triangle is used to show that the apex of conscious focal awareness has fewer potential bits of information than the nonconscious base. In the nonconscious base, stimuli are perceived, recorded, and reconstructed without awareness. Some stimuli can be readily represented consciously, whereas other stimuli are less available to reflection. Some memories are easy to retrieve with conscious intention, and others are not. In this varied nonconscious zone are huge storehouses of information and the immense

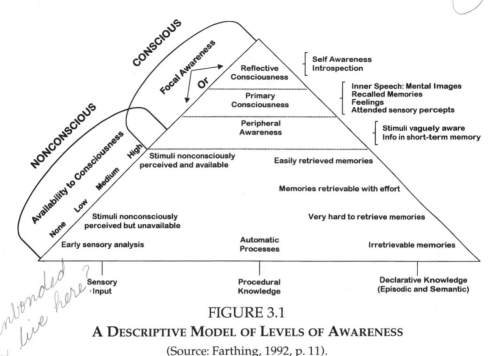

FIGURE 3.1

A DESCRIPTIVE MODEL OF LEVELS OF AWARENESS

(Source: Farthing, 1992, p. 11).

computing powers of the mind. Nevertheless, fewer bits of information does not necessarily signify less complexity; in fact, the opposite is true. Patterning in reflective consciousness is often quite complex. Conscious thought can be very highly organized, with differentiated, cross-connected, and beautifully linked associational sequences.

Most unconscious knowledge begins with the establishment of simple associational linkages. Like Pavlov's (1928–1941) dogs, humans can place additional importance on the sound of a bell that occurs before mealtime than one that occurs at random. Combinations of simple linkages produce more intricate associations; eventually, a complex network of associated meanings develops.

Complex networks of associated meanings for memory, ideas, and feelings are stored in multiple systems. As information ascends from unconscious processing to reflective conscious awareness, the mind combines input from these multiple systems. Smaller systems combine some bits of information, and then from these combinations, larger systems construct incipient conscious thoughts. In other words, initial patterns of association are aggregated into larger networks. At the level of awareness, large-scale concepts, such as self and other, are experienced.

Suppose, as an example of multiple systems, that a person is walking in the park at twilight. He or she consciously sees an ambiguous shape moving in the bushes. During a nonconscious activation of associational linkages, several alternatives are immediately primed to interpret the meaning of the moving shape to the self. These alternative interpretations of the shape occur in smaller systems that operate quickly. Because several associative networks operate on the initial incoming stimuli at more or less the same time, they can be said to be operating as *parallel processors* (Allport, 1955; Hebb, 1968; Johnson-Laird, 1988a,b). It takes many unconscious parallel processors to construct just one episode of awareness (Squire, 1986; Tulving, 1985). Processors produce different concepts; some concepts are enlarged, intensified, or repeated in the constructions of meaning that become conscious awareness. One emerging concept could be of a dangerous mugger, another of the wind blowing the branches, and yet a third of a good friend coming to the park. Conscious awareness then compares the perceptual information (the moving shapes) with the emerging concepts, and decides whether the shape is foe, branches, or friend. If, after analysis and reassessment of the stimuli, the shape could be a mugger, then conscious thought would immediately determine the next course of action.

Such clearly reportable concepts as "I thought it was a mugger, so I turned back" are recalled in a way that can be readily repeated in contemplation or by communication. This is called *declarative knowledge*, and it includes recorded information that can reconstruct specific episodes of past experience (Baddeley, 1990; Squires, 1969). Some associative networks contain knowledge about how to do something—how to turn around and run out of the park, for example. These unconscious associations are called *procedural knowledge*, and they lead to such automatic action sequences as running, playing the piano, or typing. Activation of procedural knowledge often takes place without reflective conscious awareness. Declarative knowledge can produce explicit information; procedural knowledge is more implicit. Many social exchanges use procedural knowledge. People often know implicitly how to act and react, but they may not be able to translate their actions into words.

The associational patterns within declarative and procedural knowledge are quite complex. The pattern of associational linkages between bits of information is called a *schema*. The various patterns made by these associations differentiate one schema from another, even if some of the same bits of information are in the alternative schemas.

SCHEMA

A schema, sometimes referred to as a cognitive map, simplifies detail in order to reveal an organization of interrelated meanings (Bartlett, 1932; Piaget, 1930). It is a model: Only the most salient information is given, and the less important information is omitted. A schema is a generalization, a framework likely to be useful for forming interpretations and plans.

Every mind has a repertoire of schemas for particular types of information processing. Some schemas, for example, establish the spatial relationship between objects, and others organize the sequential flow of action between objects, such as the organization of a ping-pong game. Elements in a repertoire, when activated, contribute information, (Bartlett, 1932; Horowitz, 1977a; Piaget, 1930; Rummelhart, McClelland, & PDP Research Group, 1986).

Within a repertoire of schemas, smaller-order schemas can be associatively combined into larger-order schemas (for example, combining schemas for recognizing noses and eyes into a schema of the face). In other words, schemas can be grouped into hierarchically organized sets of complicated associational networks. A *supraordinate schema* is a model of how several schemas fit together. It serves as an umbrella, covering and combining information from subordinate schemas.

PERSON SCHEMAS

Models of how aspects of the self fit together, how others are organized, and how the self affiliates with others are called *person schemas*. Person schemas are formed as knowledge is gained about the self and about others who are important to the self. Many types of schemas are person schemas: self schemas, schemas of other, role-relationship models, and critic schemas, to name a few. *Self schemas* combine many meanings that can culminate in a sense of identity. Schemas of another person—*other schemas*—construct a known figure within the mind. *Role-relationship models* articulate attachments and scripts of transactions between self and others. People also evaluate themselves and others according to rules, values, and promised affiliations. This judging stance can be called a *critic schema*. All such person schemas are complex sets of stored information and associational linkages (Horowitz, 1989b, 1991b; Horowitz, Ells, Singer & Salovey, 1995; Stinson & Palmer, 1991).

Person schemas are frameworks for understanding the self and other people. Person schemas exist in repertoires. Various alternative selves are contained in these repertoires. Schemas of others contain ways of organizing information about other people. Role-relationship models contain body images, attributional beliefs, values, intentions, and expectations about the self and others (Horowitz, 1979b, 1989b). The repertoires may be subdivided by themes such as friendships, sexuality, fighting or competing, caretaking, or working.

Small meaning systems combine to form large meaning systems. Small systems in person schemas include cognitive maps of body parts or customary inflections in voice that characterize a person. In a small system, for example, a person schema would help the mind perceive the joints as part of the fingers that could be shaped into a hand gesture. A larger system would include the hand as part of a whole person conceptualization. In the smaller system, sharply angled joints could form a clenched fist; in the larger system, the clenched fist combined with other body attributes could form a schema of an angry person. Within this larger system is a hierarchy of schemas, where one might have procedural knowledge of how to act, not only generally, with an angry person, but also more specifically, with a menacing sibling. The angled joints in the smaller system of schematization are associated with other information in the larger system of schematization, such as how to be alert for and block a punch. This procedural knowledge says, in effect, how to interpret the angry person or menacing sibling, what to expect, and what to do about it. The smaller system is integrated into the larger systems.

Schematic hierarchies assemble association linkages into more complex networks. This is simplified into a diagram of just the body concepts within a person schema, in Figure 3.2. To some extent the connections between facts or beliefs are logical, as shown by the unbroken lines of association between components of a body image. There are also cross-categorical associations. These are illustrated by broken lines. That is, associations occur between modules or logical subcategories. In Figure 3.2, associative combinations of expressions

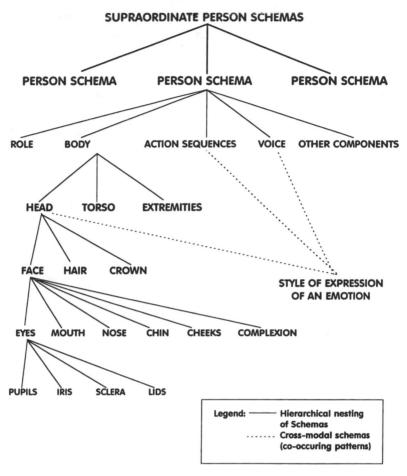

FIGURE 3.2
SCHEMATIC HIERARCHIES

that might construct an emotion are shown. For example, the anger of a brother, in an impulsive, hostile state, might be signalled by a combination of a head movement, a body gesture, and a vocal intonation. Such schematic, associatively linked, and generalized knowledge about the brother allows recognition not only of him, but of his state of mind from hearing just an inflection in his voice or seeing just a portion of his body.

Person schemas usually function outside conscious awareness. Unconscious models of a relationship influence felt emotions and, especially, longer-lasting moods. Activating an unconscious role-relationship model of a fearful, weaker self and an angry, older, and stronger sibling can organize a *tense* state of mind that is quite different from a former state of *happy play*. Yet the specific attributes of self (weak, fearful, to blame for breaking rules) and of the sibling (big fists, strong, vengeful, angry, often out of control) may not be specifically and consciously conceptualized. The emotions of apprehension may be clearer in awareness than the schematized relationship that evokes the emotions.

Person schemas evoke conscious emotional responses when they are activated during nonconscious information processing. They also evoke declarative memories, such as one of a past episode of being beaten by the sibling. The activated schemas are motivational because they generate emotional signals and influence the person's interpretation of events and actions. Inactivated or latent schemas are potentials for future intentions and expectations; they are not as motivational as the currently activated or associatively primed schemas.

not for unattached

MOTIVATION

Identity and relationship goals are important motivators. They are formed by person schemas, scripts, and unconscious intentions, as well as conscious decisions. People are inclined to activate schemas that support a positive and coherent sense of self. They are motivated to avoid awareness of self as negative, chaotic, or incompetent, and to seek future escape from present or past states that have negative identity and relationship experiences. Some people activate bad self-concepts in order to avoid the experience of chaotic states involving self-fragmentation.

People also seek good relationships and want to avoid bad ones. Their schemas inform them how to approach these goals. A desired role relationship model can be activated to evoke a positive mood. But the same acts that could begin a desired relationship could also begin a dreaded relationship. A motivational pressure might bring forth a dilemma between wish and fear. Defensive compromises could be used to avoid entering into states that are organized by dreaded schemas.

For example, Judy, a college student, was attracted to a man in her study group who also lived in her dormitory. She wanted to ask him out for coffee. She hoped he would be interested in dating her, but she also anticipated his scornful rejection. That, she believed, would humiliate her. So inviting him out could lead to either a desired state of mutual interest or the dreaded humiliation. Judy adopted a defensive stance: She decided to just study with him, without engaging in any courtship behavior.

The dynamic interplay between wishes, fears, and defenses usually operates at preconscious levels, which are close to awareness but still unconscious. In order to modify the outcome of these nonconscious processes, people can use reflective consciousness to gain insight. They can then reach new decisions on how to revise knowledge, correct errors of belief, and improve their circumstances. The new decisions usually lead to new behaviors. Repetitions of thought and behavior increase certain associational network patterns. Such repetitions are a way that people can slowly reschematize themselves. Awareness, insight, decisions, and repetitions can lead to reschematization and a revised or better integrated sense of identity. The college student might come to realize that she does not have to anticipate humiliation even if her overtures are rejected, so she might decide to take the risk.

In psychotherapy, patients often enter a state of obscurity, doubt, confusion, and avoidance when asked what they think is their best possible future. This is because placing the self in a desired future, although important, is nearly always emotionally conflictual. In very conflicted individuals, the fantasy of a desired future is linked tightly to a fantasy of a dreaded future. Wishes, if represented, can lead to representation of dire consequences. With increased awareness and reduced confusion, patients can speak more comfortably about their wish–fear dilemmas. To gain awareness and insight and make new decisions about dilemmas, the psychotherapist may encourage reflective conscious awareness. Such awareness occurs in several ways. Visual images and bodily sensations, for example, can activate emotional reactions: psychotherapy seldom proceeds on words alone.

MODES OF REPRESENTATION

Conscious thought requires different modes of representation for expressing the full pictures of a person's thoughts and feelings. The representations, and flows of representation, are organized by schemas. Bruner (1964) and Horowitz (1970) described three major categories of representation: *body enactions, mental images,* and *mental words,* as outlined in Table 3.1 (c.f. Bucci, 1985; Hunt, 1995; Paivio,

TABLE 3.1
MODES OF CONSCIOUS REPRESENTATION

Conscious Representation Mode	Subsystems	Sample Organizational Tendencies	Sample Derivative
Enactions	Musculature	Sequences of actions	Gestural imitations of an action
	Autonomic nervous system	Patterned arousal	Somatic sensations
Images	Visual	Spatial relationships and shape comparisons	Daydream
	Tactile-kinesthetic	Coordination	Sense of shrinking or enlarging
	Olfactory-gustatory	Selecting appetite relevance	Revulsion or attraction
	Auditory	Inner–outer alertings	Startle reaction
Words	Different languages	Meanings by categories	Logical deduction

1989). Each category has special properties. A specific thought is expressed differently in each category. A state of mind high in the use of visual imagery and low in the use of lexical meanings leads to a different line of contemplation on a topic than a state low in the use of visual imagery and high in the use of words. For example, pictures in the mind's eye of sandy beaches, a turquoise sea, gentle lapping waves, and soft breezes beneath a sunny sky may be more soothing than verbal thoughts of an island vacation.

Many states have seamless blends of representation. In Figure 3.3, these blends of meaning are called *integrated attention*. What is consciously represented in one mode usually seems translated freely and effortlessly into other modes of representation. A person can verbalize the images of a dream while using appropriate body language and facial expressions. However, despite the seamless blend

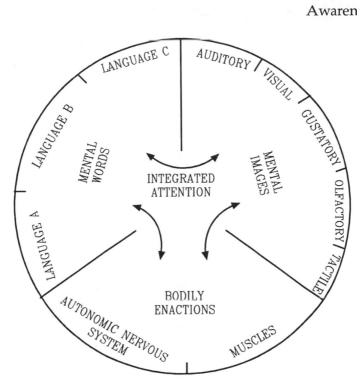

FIGURE 3.3
MODES OF REPRESENTATION

of many experiences in reflective consciousness, the construction of meanings into expressions is modular (Fodor, 1983).

Parallel processors build information in unconscious channels. The processors feed information into the representational modes. The processors and the representational modes function as specialized and separable "intelligences" (Gardner, 1985). That is, they serve as skills for linguistic, logical–mathematical, spatial, bodily–kinesthetic, and other dimensions of know-how.

Unconscious defensive control processes can inhibit or facilitate representation of specific information (content) and can inhibit or facilitate modal systems (form). Controls can also block translation from one mode to another. For example, in psychotherapy, an urge for revenge was depicted by a patient as an intrusive and intense visual image of destroying a rival's car. The motivation for thinking about this hostile action remained untranslated into words. The idea chain "I am angry at him for hurting me and want to get even by blowing up his car" was inhibited from lexical representation.

The Enactive Mode

Facial expressions and bodily gestures are enactions. People can consciously reflect on felt muscle tensions as a way of gaining information about unconscious emotional reactions to bad news (Zajonc, 1980). The stomach and throat could constrict, leading to the experience of anxiety translated lexically as "butterflies in my stomach" or "a frog in my throat." Weak knees, a pounding heart, and tightness across the chest may be reflected on and translated into "I get butterflies in my stomach when I see a fire." These associations lead to insights such as "I am afraid of fire!"

For example, a woman, while conversing, seeks to use the expression, "He likes to pin people down," but for the moment, has forgotten the phrase. While attempting to find the words and say them, she instead makes a hand gesture of pinning something down, thus enacting the usually lexical thought, which is, for the moment and for some reason, inhibited or just unavailable. The words she is seeking then enter awareness and she verbalizes them. The enactive representation facilitates the lexical concepts.

The Image Mode

There are various types of image representation, each in a sensory organizing system: visual (sight), auditory (hearing), tactile (touch), olfactory (smell), gustatory (taste), and kinesthetic (sensations of movement and position). Some people seldom think in visual images, and 5% of a normal population say they never do (McKellar, 1957; Pylyshyn, 1984, 1994). Whereas some people have visual thought images that are only fleeting and have only a partial or dim sensory quality, others sometimes experience conscious thought as a series of detailed, color intense images (Kosslyn, 1981; Singer, 1966). Sometimes these flows of visualization even seem like uncontrolled movies or scintillations of a scattered dream during waking life (Horowitz, 1983a).

The formation of images is a process of construction as the mind's many parallel processors combine, compare, and recombine sets of information (Kosslyn, 1994). Image formation allows an individual to contemplate objects that are absent. Adeptness with visual images is useful to architects, painters, and surgeons. Skill at auditory image formation is useful in poetry and music; kinesthetic imagery is useful in dance choreography; olfactory and gustatory imagery is useful in devising new recipes for cooking.

Analysts—including Joseph Breuer and Sigmund Freud ([1895] 1955), Carl Jung (1959), Lawrence Kubie (1943), and Roberto Assagioli (1965)—have suggested to their patients that they utilize visual imagery in order to facilitate free association. This use of pictorial thought seems to reduce defensive control of emotion (Bucci, 1997; Ferenczi, 1950; Jung, 1939, 1959). Guided imagery has become a technique in various schools of psychotherapy (Horowitz, 1983a; Pope & Singer, 1978).

A conscious visual image combines information from external stimuli and internal schemas. One example is the visualization of a blueprint as a three-dimensional room. The conscious representation is forged from both information in the drawing and schemas of knowledge about the structure of a room.

Figure 3.4 illustrates the multiple sources of information used in forming an image. Processors combine incoming perceptual stimuli with memory of prior perceptions and conscious images, as well as input from activated associational linkages and schemas. Translations from other modes of representation are also added during the construction of a conscious image (Schacter & Tulving, 1994; see Figure 3.4).

The important aspect of this figure is that any conscious representation is the result of a constructive process of converged and combined meanings. The mind is not a camera that always takes true-to-life visual snapshots and then repeats them. Memories are difficult to stamp as true or false because any current awareness is a construction derived from a combination of inputs (Butler & Spiegel, 1997).

THE LEXICAL MODE

At first, sounds are used for communication, such as when a baby babbles to its mother. Eventually, a relationship is established between words and the objects and actions they signify. Different language systems such as English and Spanish may exist in separate associational networks (as shown in Figure 3.3). Translations occur between different systems; this is a more complex and differentiated process than thinking within a single system.

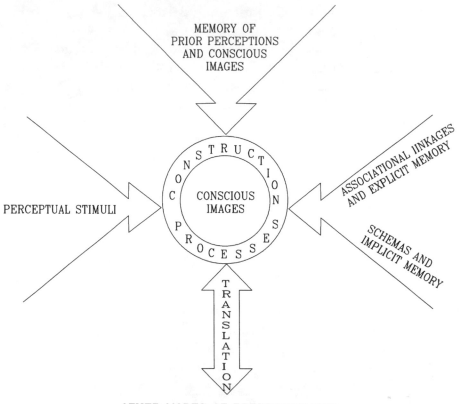

FIGURE 3.4
FORMING AN IMAGE

Construction of meaning in word sequences requires temporal ordering, just as visual representation requires spatial ordering. The acquisition of lexical representation adds a new dimension to conscious thought. As people develop, they become more competent at abstract generalizations, reasoning, and planning of complex and orderly sequences (Jackendoff, 1987). New levels of understanding the self and the environment are fostered by the acquisition of lexical capacity.

EMOTIONAL INSIGHT

Emotional relationships involve a complex set of social and personal meanings. Many of the transactions that people want and fear are processed nonconsciously. Developing insight requires both a reduction of defensive obscurities and a declaration of ideas and feelings into multimodal representation. By multimodal representation, complex medleys of feeling and desire, of plans and fears, can be deeply understood. The person can translate unconscious attitudes into words, images, and enactions, and can then examine contradictory beliefs and decide how to resolve conflicts.

In self-analysis and psychotherapy, people usually have to declare emotion in words as well as images. They often use complex emotional words such as pride, shame, guilt, envy, longing, and self-pity. These words are complex because they imply interpersonal attitudes. Their meaning needs to be unpacked in order for awareness and insight to deepen. This refinement requires the person to explicitly state the concepts about self and others that are associated with an emotion. Envy, for example, contains the desire for an object, frustration at not having it, anger at a person who gives the object to another, jealousy of the person getting the object, and perhaps disgust at the self for being without it.

Insight into a feeling such as envy involves many representations of ideas, as illustrated in the case of Judy. This is not an actual case history; it composites observations from several real cases into a fictional example.

CASE STUDY: JUDY

Judy, as discussed earlier, is the college student who wanted to date a man in her dormitory and study group. She had a history of being shy around men, expecting them to reject and humiliate her by scorning any interest she might have in them. The man in question had looked at her with interest on several occasions, in a way that indicated he, also, was shy, but possibly wanted to date her. Other women in the study group flirted with him in a way that Judy envied. He was hesitant to make the first move, but he looked at Judy briefly whenever some other woman was flirting with him.

Judy feigned indifference as a defensive stance against the wish–fear dilemma: If she expressed interest, she might get what she wanted, but she might also be rejected and feel ashamed. She had indeed sought psychotherapy to work out reasons for her intense envy of other women and defensive avoidances of engaging in age appropriate behaviors with men.

One day, Karen sat next to this man. Judy had long envied Karen for her self-possessed and bold stance, as well as her physical attractiveness. Karen and the man engaged in an animated discussion before the class started, and Judy felt envy as well as self-disgust for not acting like Karen. Awareness of such negative emotions was a part of the work she had done with her therapist. What follows is an unpacking of some aspects of these negative emotions, including Judy's envy of Karen.

In therapy, Judy used her visual images of Karen. In her mind's eye, she imagined Karen and translated what she saw into words, calling Karen poised, good-looking, and courageous. Then Judy imitated what she saw and what she labeled. Using enactive representation, Judy achieved poised, animated, and vivacious postures and facial expressions. This was a trial identification with Karen's admired traits.

Judy visually represented her own face and compared it with Karen's. She felt that her face was less appealing and lexically labeled Karen as prettier. Judy then imagined herself in Karen's place, sitting beside the man. She felt a flush of anger at the idea that Karen had usurped her. An enactive representation of her anger was derived from the change in muscles and blood vessels and the feeling of heat in her face. She labeled this sensation in words associated with anger.

Using reflective consciousness, Judy was able to say at this point that she felt envy. Then she reported how she disliked feeling envious. She was even aware of an incipient defense. She said she was about to say, "He was not really very interesting." Instead of leaving the topic, she stayed with it, and admitted how interested she was in this man. Judy imagined herself being vivacious just like Karen. She remembered a photograph of herself smiling brightly just before her high school prom. She then decided to make her own plans; she decided to introduce herself in the next class, and she planned to stop feigning indifference.

Judy's awareness, aided by different models of representation, led to insight. Insight, aided by the use of reflective consciousness, led to new choices, plans, and behaviors. The safe relationship in therapy, and conscious intentions to develop insight, led her from feigned indifference to a direct, well-modulated display of interest.

Judy's social change had its micromoment during a psychotherapy session. When she found herself wanting to say, "He was not that interesting," she consciously counteracted her disavowal; instead, she elaborated on her interest in him. Using insight about her envy, she decided on traits she wanted to practice for herself. She was not going to copy Karen exactly; she decided to develop her own kind of poise and assertiveness.

Awareness and conceptual work in reflective consciousness helped Judy gain insight. She could then make decisions on how and what to change. She tried out new behaviors. She paid attention to finding out what worked best. That, in turn, led to changes in her identity: She felt more effective and her relationship patterns improved. These progressive changes in behavior had revised her person schemas.

MEMORIES AND INTRUSIONS INTO AWARENESS

Memories consist of complex sets of stored information, connected by associational networks. Recall of a memory to conscious awareness requires a constructive process. When a memory is about an episode that just occurred, fewer constructive processes are needed to bring it to awareness. When a memory is about an episode that occurred further away from current awareness, more constructive processes are required to retrieve it. Short-term memories, in other words, are easier to recall and have less insertion of other contents from parallel processors (J. Anderson, 1983; Bower, 1981; Kosslyn, 1994; Neisser, 1988; Squires, 1969).

Short-term memories sometimes press for representation in conscious awareness, even without volitional effort. Anyone driving for a long time at night might, on trying to sleep, have images of oncoming headlights. After picking berries all day, images of berries may return as unbidden pictures later on in the mind's eye. Usually such effects subside fairly quickly, and they are probably due to activation and deactivation of schemas as well as repetitions from short-term memories. But sometimes memories intrude again and again, even after a long period of apparent forgetfulness. For this reason, some memory storage—called *active memory storage*—is regarded as having a special propensity for repeated representation. Traumatic memories and even traumatic dreams and fantasies can recur in this manner: They intrude unbidden into awareness despite the opposing control processes (Horowitz, 1972, 1977b).

Very important experiences are likely to be stored in active memory for later reconsideration. Some important topics in active memory (for example, traumatic events) are associated with dreaded states. Repeated conscious representation of uncontrollable emotional distress is nonconsciously anticipated. These topics in active memory are then inhibited from representation to avoid undermodulated emotion. But the active memories are so primed that stimuli are too easily linked associatively to them. Such stimuli then trigger intrusive recollections, or even flashbacks (Horowitz, 1969).

Perceptions and associations to these perceptions can prime memories in active memory storage. The opposing forces—associative priming and defensive inhibition—combine in different ways to produce a variety of states. A balance of forces heavily favoring inhibition tends to lead to an overmodulated state. When the balance shifts, due to priming or lapse in inhibition, often warded-off mental contents gain conscious representation. A sense of intrusion then occurs: The images are unbidden, the enactions are unwanted. The person then tends to enter an undermodulated state. To reduce emotion aroused by the images and enactions, the person may still inhibit words that label the experiences with semantic clarity. The combination can tend to cause the person to manifest a shimmering state.

Intrusions, even in an unpleasant and undermodulated state, may begin a process that leads to insight.

FRED: AN EXAMPLE OF UNBIDDEN VISUAL IMAGES AFTER A STRESSOR LIFE EVENT

Unbidden images tormented Fred, age 25, after the suicide of his friend Gregory. A few days before the suicide, Gregory, who seemed very depressed, telephoned Fred and asked him to come over and be with him. Fred said he did not have the time to get together. When he later heard that Gregory had committed suicide, Fred said to himself, "I refuse to feel guilty about that," and put all ideas about Gregory out of his conscious mind. A week later, intrusive images of Gregory's face occurred whenever Fred shut his eyes; he could sleep only with the lights on. He dreaded the recurrences of these threatening images to such an extent that he changed the way he washed his face: He washed in such a way that he didn't have to close his eyes to keep out the soap. Finally, when he could no longer deny his emotional reaction to Gregory's suicide, he discussed the problem in psychotherapy and came to both accept and work through his feelings of guilt.

When warded-off contents intrude into awareness, the person feels a lapse in control because the experience was not expected. A sense of entering an undermodulated or shimmering state of mind occurs. Shifts from well-modulated into undermodulated or shimmering states may be symptomatic of unresolved conflicts. Resolving the conflict reduces the frequency of these alterations. In the case of Fred, the unresolved conflict involved a social event, the suicide of a friend. On the one hand, his mind tended to then engage important questions such as Who was to blame? Who could have prevented the death? What will others say about me now? On the other hand, Fred did not want to experience bad feelings or negative self-appraisals. He wanted to go on with his planned activities. His undermodulated state of intrusive images occurred partly because of his conflicted intentions, whether or not to think about the suicide. This state was more likely to occur when his attention was less focused on other topics, when he let his mind rest, and when he was physically fatigued. After a period of time, Fred was less defensive; he contemplated the suicide, his own role, and his own self-criticism. As he worked through his reactions to the suicide, the topic became a more dormant and less intrusive memory.

WORKING MODELS

Working through a stressful event—such as the news of his friend's suicide, in Fred's case—requires more than remembrance of the prior experiences. The ideas and feelings that are the central contents of awareness both influence and are influenced by active cognitive maps. Such maps or schemas organize the sequential association of ideas and feelings and are themselves sometimes self-observable in reflective consciousness. These active, close-to-awareness maps can be called *working models* because such schemas lead to work-products: new decisions about what to believe, what new attitude to take, and what choices to make. Working models, as shown in Figure 3.5, transact with the contents of awareness and with activated schemas within a repertoire of stored schemas.

Working models combine information from perception, thought, and emotions with information from prior schematizations. They foster rapid decision making. Derivatives of working models are more accessible to reflective consciousness than are derivatives from enduring schemas.

The more active schemas lead to a working model. Once activated, schemas can contribute erroneous information. A check on input,

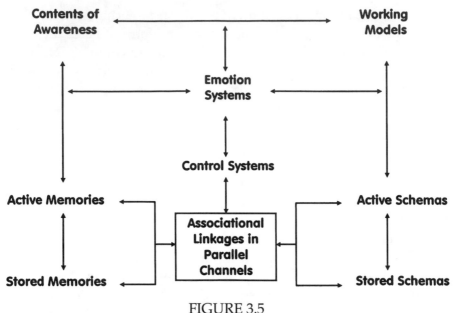

FIGURE 3.5

EMERGING CONTENTS AND PARALLEL PROCESSING

through reappraisal and reinterpretation, can correct the error and change a working model. (Janis, 1969; Lazarus, 1966, 1991). The startling illusion of seeing a dead friend may be corrected to seeing a stranger with some resembling features. The desire to see the friend as alive may have contributed a motive to the formation of the illusion. Understanding that motive can lead to insight into why such illusions may be repeated.

Nonconscious mental processes involve both stored memories (such as episodes of prior experience) and stored schemas that are periodically activated. This is also shown in Figure 3.5. Both of these larger meaning units, memories and schemas, affect information processing. Different parallel processors form different patterns of associational linkage. These processors influence awareness, and conversely, awareness influences the processors.

There are top-down and bottom-up effects, as shown in Figure 3.5. Both reflective consciousness and unconscious information processing can activate emotion systems. Emotional systems then co-determine what happens next during information processing (Lazarus, 1991). Mismatches between contents of awareness and what was expected may be especially potent in evoking emotions. Emotions affect the associational networks that evoke a working model.

Emotions also affect processors that, like the thermostat of a furnace, regulate feeling states. In other words, emotional control is yet another aspect of information processing. To avoid emotional flooding, some control systems can regulate the activation or inhibition of associational networks. Controls can alter ideas, beliefs, fantasies, memories, schemas, perceptions, and actions.

To prevent dreaded out-of-control states, some information processing can be blocked. Parallel processors can be inhibited and the gateways to conscious representational modes impeded. These complex transactional influences on information processing are shown by the notation "control systems" in Figure 3.5. The processes of control that can alter the contents of awareness are considered in detail in the next chapter.

SUMMARY

In order to understand awareness of thoughts and feelings, one has to infer a complex and interactive network of unconsciously processed information. Memories, fantasies, schemas, emotions, and controls transact with current perceptions to form the stream of experience. An extraordinary human ability occurs when, in reflective consciousness, the person can split awareness into an experiencing self and an observing self. The latter can infer the reasons for some otherwise mysterious experiences.

Sometimes defensive control processes have to be altered to achieve awareness. Controls can inhibit enactive, image, and lexical information-processing systems. In well-modulated states, people usually shift from one mode to heighten another. Sometimes, shifting to visual imagery in reflective consciousness can safely bring up otherwise warded-off ideas and feelings. Almost all schools of psychotherapy employ image-forming techniques to reduce defensiveness, but only a few use enaction-forming techniques because of the dangers of acting on the intense emotional impulses that may erupt.

Defensive control processes can diminish awareness and avoid anticipated, dreaded, highly emotional states. In the short run, this avoidance of feeling can be adaptive—it can lead to cool decision-making. Habitual over-control of emotion, however, can limit personal development and leave conflicts unresolved. For this reason, to increase insight and facilitate new decisions, psychotherapy often involves attention to controls.

CHAPTER 4

Control of Emotion

M ANY IDEAS and feelings are processed unconsciously and do not achieve representation in reflective consciousness. Often these remain unconscious because more immediate or important thoughts and emotions occupy the available modes for conscious representation; no particular mental activities are preventing them from gaining attention. Sometimes specific memories and fantasies are blocked from awareness. Such inhibition is usually for the purposes of warding off ideas, feelings and urges that might lead to a dreaded state of mind. The mental activity used to prevent unwanted arousals of emotion is defensive in nature. Such defenses can be adaptive in that they prevent the danger of emotional flooding, but they can also be maladaptive because they prevent a full recognition of ideas and can blunt the possibilities for solutions to difficult problems.

Psychoanalysis and the initial work of Sigmund Freud emphasized defenses using the term *repression* (Breuer & Freud, 1895; Freud, 1900). Repression was the unconscious stifling of memories, fantasies, urges, ideas, and feelings that otherwise would gain conscious representation. It turned out, however, that there were many ways by which such avoidances could be achieved. That is why Freud (1914a, 1920a, 1923) began to delineate other mechanisms of defense, and his daughter Anna Freud (1936) compiled one of the first sets of definitions for these processes. Later clinicians and academic scholars interpreted and described a variety of defense mechanisms. Clinical research led to more reliable definitions and established the validity of these unconscious defensive operations (Conte & Plutchik, 1995; Cooper, 1992; Cramer, 1991; Haan, 1977; Hentschel, Smith, Ehlers, & Draguns, 1993; Perry & Kardos, 1995; Vaillant, 1992, 1993, 1994). Although the essential concepts have been well studied, a satisfactory categorization of defenses has not been agreed on. A new theory was indicated and has since emerged, based on cognitive psychodynamics. Its categorization has been based on research efforts focused on self-ratings and on observer ratings of how people control emotion, especially when under stress (Horowitz, 1977a, 1988b; Horowitz, Cooper, et al., 1992; Horowitz, Markman, Stinson, Ghannam, & Fridhandler, 1990; Horowitz, Milbrath, & Stinson, 1995; Horowitz & Stinson, 1995; Horowitz, Znoj, & Stinson, 1996).

Different authors use terms for stress, coping, and defense in different ways. In this book, *stress* refers to events and situations that cause a strain. *Coping* refers to strategies used to reduce stress (Zeidner & Endler, 1995). *Defense* refers to processes that ward off dreaded emotional arousal. For example, after the death of a loved one, a person copes by seeking the support of friends, planning the funeral, handling finances, and finding time for self-restoration through contemplation. After such a loss, the person might cope within a normal range of affect or with defensive avoidance of feeling: He or she might feel and manifest emotions such as appropriate anger and sadness, or conversely, not display any emotion at all. In this numb state, the person might not know that his or her emotions are being blunted by defensive control processes, and the person might not be aware of what he or she is warding off from full experience.

DEFENSIVE CONTROL PROCESSES

To reduce emotional arousal, some controls shift thought contents. Others alter the form of thought. Still other defensive control processes shift the person schemas that knit information together. The following example shows how such defensive control processes stifle emotion and omit important insights, yet serve functional purposes. The combination of several control processes helped Sophia to cope with and adapt to a highly stressful event.

SOPHIA

Sophia, a woman with beauty and grace, made an excellent living as a sought-after model. A car accident resulted in injuries that required amputation of one of her legs; she also emerged with severe facial scarring and permanent blindness. She spent months in hospital and convalescent home treatment.

Initially, Sophia had to be fed by another person, but at this point in her recovery, she did not let herself become aware of her blindness; she would not discuss the topic. She did think and talk about the loss of her leg. Her lack of recognition of being blind was astonishing to staff members because of her utter dependence on them.

Only after several weeks passed did her awareness of being blind emerge. She addressed the topic of her facial disfigurement and loss of a career even later. It was as if she had made an unconscious choice that she could and would cope with just one terrible theme at a time.

Each change in her body meant a change to her future and her sense of identity; each change was very distressing. Sophia was periodically tearful, frightened, and angry, but was not overwhelmed; she was able to keep out of her current awareness topics that were just too much to bear. She seemed unaware that she had unconsciously organized defensive control processes to blunt emotion. These regulatory strategies protected her from disorganization and despair. As equilibrium was restored, the important topics, although painful, could be contemplated in a tolerable, dose-by-dose-manner.

Immediately after her bodily losses, Sophia had not yet had time to develop self schemas and bodily concepts to accord to the new realities. Her new body sensations did not match her expectations. The discordancy was alarming, and she had to progressively learn to tolerate the emotional arousals and to revise her body schemas and other self-concepts. Such a general process of matching new representations in awareness with unconscious expectations is shown in Figure 4.1. Only when Sophia had revised her beliefs about self could she disengage her attention from her new bodily sensations without being defensive.

Figure 4.1 shows how incongruencies lead to reappraisal and revision of new information and preexisting beliefs. Figure 4.2 shows how incongruencies can evoke emotional alarm reactions. To avoid the danger of entering into a dreaded state, a person like Sophia can activate defensive control processes. Ideas that evoke negative emotions are then inhibited. Alternative concepts may be facilitated in

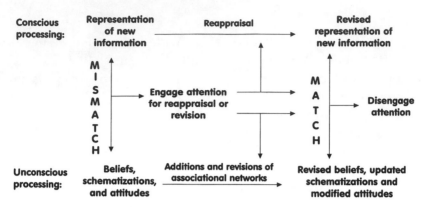

FIGURE 4.1

INFORMATION PROCESSING: REAPPRAISAL AND REVISION
AFTER A MISMATCH

order to shift attention away from the dreaded concepts. The entire
process can be unconscious (Freud, 1923; Lang, 1994; Ledoux, 1995).

STEVE

Steve, a surgical resident, was at a crucial level of training, one that
would dictate his future career. Steve's goal was to become a great
surgeon. His attending surgeon told Steve that he was not meeting
the required standards of skill.

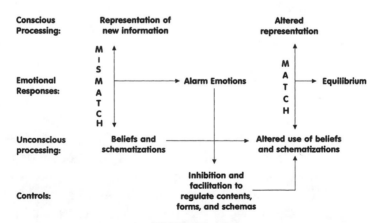

FIGURE 4.2

INFORMATION PROCESSING: MISMATCH LEADS TO EMOTION
AND EFFORTS TO CONTROL EMOTION

The new information—that he had only mediocre skills in a key area—was in sharp discord with Steve's goal. He believed that he did have great skill and had to be a surgeon to be worthwhile. The mismatch threatened self-esteem; Steve anticipated entering, as he had in the past, a dreaded state of excessive humiliation. His sense of mortal degradation could lead to suicidal preoccupations. To avoid this dreaded excessive humiliation state, Steve activated defensive control processes that inhibited criticism on the topic of surgical skills from contemplation.

Steve's defensive avoidance could be categorized in a number of ways, depending on the chosen classification theory. One way is the classical psychoanalytic terminology of *defensive mechanisms*. If his avoidance of the surgical skills topic was a conscious choice, then Steve's acts would be called *suppression*. If it was an unconsciously chosen inhibition that "could and should" become conscious, then it would be called *repression*. In the present theory, the relevant processes involve *inhibition of a topic*.

Steve shuffled the priorities of various topics for conscious contemplation. His next topic of awareness was always some topic other than what his attending surgeon had said about his skill. Other topics were facilitated as the skill topic was inhibited. Figure 4.3 illus-

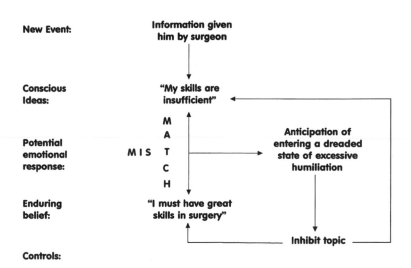

FIGURE 4.3
INFORMATION PROCESSING: STEVE'S ANTICIPATION
OF INTENSE EMOTION AND INHIBITION OF TOPIC

trates Steve's topic inhibition and the interactions of his ideas, emotions, and controls. He withheld the skill topic to avoid humiliation. The inhibitory aim opposed any tendency to recall the memory about the criticism; it also hesitated in making any decision as to how Steve might cope with this important and unintegrated experience.

Whereas inhibition of topics can affect the contents of awareness, another control process can affect the form of awareness. Image representation, for example, could be inhibited and only lexical representation permitted. By inhibiting his image representation, Steve could avoid visual fantasies of others looking scornfully on his failure. Another kind of control can alter person schemas. Steve could inhibit conceptualizing himself as a degraded man, and, instead, facilitate concepts of himself as a competent man in another career. Figure 4.4 illustrates how Steve's decision to be an anesthesiologist was associated with a shift from a degraded to a competent self schema. Steve could also alter schemas of his attending surgeon by shifting away from viewing him as an admired competent mentor to viewing him as an incompetent judge. Although Steve might be unaware of using these defensive shifts in person schemas, the result would affect his emotional state.

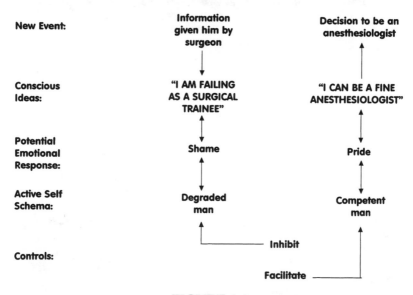

FIGURE 4.4

Information Processing: Steve's Inhibition and Facilitation of Self Schemas

When people like Sophia or Steve receive dire news, their minds require time for assimilation and accommodation. Dose-by-dose contemplation often occurs, as emotional arousals from mismatches are regulated by defensive control processes, coping strategies, and social supports. Between doses of emotional contemplation, the important topic is latent in regard to conscious awareness, but is active in unconscious associations of ideas and feelings.

Each dose of contemplation can accomplish some work. As a result of that work, emotional reactions, and especially, alarm reactions, are less likely to occur. As an outcome reminders trigger memories without causing an entry into dreaded and undermodulated states of mind. Control processes are used less extremely, more for coping and less for totally avoidant defensive stances.

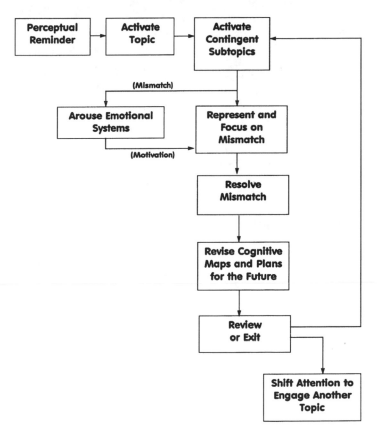

FIGURE 4.5
CONTEMPLATION OF A TOPIC

This course of mastery involves the many subtopics connected by associational linkages to the main topic. For example, a stressor event leads to vivid memories and also begins a cascade of ideation on its implications to the self and to relationship bonds. A reminder of the event tends to activate not just the memory but the process of contemplating the related subtopics, especially those with important but unsolved problems.

Figure 4.5 outlines the general course of review of topics and subtopics. Repetition is the important aspect of such review. When a topic or subtopic has already been contemplated repeatedly, the next reviews may proceed more and more rapidly, and with fewer or less intense emotional alarms if the prior reviews included work to resolve problems, revise schemas, and make new plans or cognitive maps.

A CLASSIFICATION OF CONTROL PROCESSES

There are three broad categories for controlling emotions: *control of contents of conscious experience, control of form of thought,* and *control of person schemas.* Each broad category has several types of control. Some of these were introduced in the cases of Sophia and Steve and are now examined in more detail.

CONTROLLING CONTENTS OF CONSCIOUS EXPERIENCE

The contents of awareness can be selected by the following processes: *controlling topics* by shifting from one topic to another, *altering concepts* by shifting from one set of concepts to another, *altering the importance of a chain of concepts to the self* by shifting from one chain to another, and *altering the threshold for disengagement* of a topic by prematurely ending its contemplation.

Altering Topics

Various systems of memory retain information. Some memories in storage function as lists of important but unfinished topics; these are active memories, ones that tend to be repeated in representation. Active memories have an intrinsic tendency to regain attention in focal consciousness. Traumatic memories and anxious fantasies are prime examples.

Potential topics stored in active memory storages can be selectively inhibited or facilitated by control processes. The topic priority for conscious attention can change. Changing a priority may lead to a shift in awareness from thinking about one topic to contemplating another (Uleman & Borgs, 1989; Wegner & Pennebaker, 1993). One topic is disengaged, attention shifts, and a new topic is engaged (Posner, 1990).

Inhibiting an important topic, as illustrated in Steve's case (Figure 4.3) can have adaptive and maladaptive outcomes. Emotional equilibrium is preserved by inhibition, and another topic can then be contemplated. Maladaptively, postponement can lead to pathological levels of forgetting, disavowal, or denial of stressful topics that require decisions about the best way to cope. It can prevent a resolution of internal conflicts about future goals for self and others. By excessively inhibiting the topic of the criticism of his surgical skills, Steve might never work through the memory, might never think through his best pathway for the future.

Altering Concepts

Concepts are ideas that are chained together to produce a conscious sequence of thought about a particular topic. For example, Sophia, who had lost a leg, might be thinking consciously about the topic of what this might mean in regard to her employment. She might have a series of chains of concepts that could be simplified into desired, dreaded, problematic compromise, and quasi-adaptive compromise, as follows:

Desired sequence.   "My leg is gone. As a model, I need it to stand and to walk. I need my job. They want me to go to physical therapy and practice with an artificial leg. Maybe I can learn to use it well. I will take my time and practice carefully. I have done other hard things; I can do this one. I will do as they suggest."

Dreaded sequence.   "My leg is gone. As a model, I need it to stand and to walk. I need my job. They want me to go to physical therapy and practice with an artificial leg. That will never work. I will be unable to work. I will be rejected and scorned. My life is ruined. I hate myself and them. I won't comply. I will turn my face to the wall and die."

Problematic compromise.   My leg is gone and I need it. I cannot face
   this right now. I will tell them I am too upset for the physical
   therapy. Maybe a long time from now I will reconsider. For
   the time being I'll just sign out of the hospital and live in a
   wheelchair."

Quasi-adaptive compromise.   "My leg is gone and I need it. Walking
   with an artificial limb seems really hard and is much less than
   I want. But it is the best thing available under the circumstances. I cannot fully face imagining the future without my
   leg right now. But I can agree to go out and try out the artificial limb. I'll give it a try just today and think about the rest
   later."

Ideas and feelings are interactive during the chaining of a set of
concepts into a train of thought. Ideational and emotional systems
transact and are organized by unconscious beliefs and schemas, past
memories and fantasies, goals, and long-standing fears. In a pre-existing depressed mode, ideas might chain more pessimistically than
in a mood of greater vitality. However, ideas connected into an opti-
mistic sequence might lighten feelings of sadness.

Associative memories are part of these determinants. Certain
chains of concepts are associated with entry, in the past, into dreaded
states of mind. These concepts are the ones most likely to be automatically, that is unconsciously, inhibited at the gateway to one of
the modes for conscious representation. In psychotherapy, and in
self-developing reflective consciousness, intentions are formed to
counteract these automatic inhibitions and to become aware of the
warded-off ideas and feelings.

Each concept, and each link of that concept to other beliefs, is constructed into conscious representation from nonconscious sources of information. The processes that form conscious concepts are themselves
unconscious. At these unconscious levels, information can be processed
in parallel. Alternative concepts are activated and linked in parallel
processors. As the gateway to conscious representation is reached, only
some concepts are active enough to emerge. In leading up to this selec-
tion, some processors are enhanced and others inhibited.

Unconscious activities anticipate the possible consequences of
adding a particular concept into a line of thought. Unconscious
thought is a precursor to and a trial of conscious thought. Useless,
relatively unimportant, erroneous, or dangerous concepts such as,

"My life is entirely ruined so I hate everyone," may be discontinued before they are consciously represented.

As chains of conscious thought occur, appraisals about them also occur. These appraisals range from value judgments such as "I like that idea!" or "that scares me!" to logical estimates such as "that could solve the problem." Such evaluations influence what concepts will be repeated when the topic is re-examined in conscious thought. When the chain of concepts about a topic is repeated, some elements in the chain of ideas may be dropped out and others substituted.

Difficult choices usually require repeated episodes of conscious contemplation, with many alterations in how concepts are chained into a train of thought. Sometimes these alterations have different purposes. At times they are defensive, to avoid dreaded emotional arousals. At other times they are adaptive efforts to come up with a better solution to a problem. Tight, logical linkages of concepts can lead to clarity in thought; loose associations can lead to confusion. On the other hand, a broad and free range of active association, one that allows leaps and flights, can lead to a stunning, creative insight.

Insight and new decisions nearly always require repeated contemplations. This is a time when alternative conceptual connections are used in conscious thought, and when parallel nonconscious processors are allowed to bring in more remote rather than tightly reasoned linkages of associated ideas. These repetitions, and appraisals of value of self and others, have an important additional effect: They revise the associational networks. That is, the linkage strengths between associated ideas and feelings are modified. A connection can become stronger and is more likely to occur; another connection can become relatively weak and is less likely to gain representation in the future. This process is one of reschematization: The patterns of belief are being changed during the assessments.

Defensive shifts in the chaining together of ideas can diminish the seeming relevance of a topic to the self; it is boring rather than difficult. Defensiveness can also block the processes of adaptive reschematizations. Relevant but challenging emotional concepts are omitted in favor of irrelevant but safe details. The excessive use of such controls, in the short run, can interrupt a course of contemplation that could master traumatic life experiences. Habitual use of such inhibition can lead to a thought style of generalization, intellectualization, and disavowal. Disavowal occurs when a counteractive concept is amplified to mask one that is emotionally challenging.

It is interesting to note that jokes often involve shifts from anticipated sequences of concepts. For a spontaneous laugh to occur, a surprising change is necessary. In a cartoon, one is supposed to look at the picture, and then at the caption. The picture activates associations and several possible models of understanding. Likely concepts are then altered by the punchline. If the picture activates fear, the caption can suddenly reduce the threat and relieve the tension. For example, a cartoon shows a hooded figure of the grim reaper of death in the doorway; a person is answering the door. The caption above the grim reaper is "Don't worry, I've just come for your toaster." The picture activates terror of death; the caption shifts to a trivial loss.

Altering the Importance of a Chain of Concepts to the Self

When consciously considered, a chain of ideas can be appraised for its importance to one's existing self-regard and for its pertinence to personal intentions and expectations. A chain of ideas that solves a problem may be ranked high in importance. That chain can be followed by another problem-solving chain. Reflective conscious awareness can compare these two alternative solutions. Each chain is weighed for its relative importance. One can be chosen over the other, or new combinations can be made and better solutions found.

By shifting the value attached to a chain of concepts, a person can alter which chain influences the next thought. This process affects choices. The significance of a chain of ideas to one's possible future, for example, can be exaggerated or minimized. Associational strengths between concepts can be augmented or reduced. This shift in importance can lead to adaptive, rational evaluations. It can also lead to maladaptive, irrational meanings; excessive attitudes and exaggerated expectations of futures for the self may be formed. Excessive magnification can result in irrational idealization and excessive minimizations in devaluation. Devaluation and idealization can lead to rationalizations for deciding to stay with second-rate lemons by calling them sweet and giving up a longing for first-rate grapes by calling them sour.

In the previous example, Steve repeated the memory of the senior surgeon telling him that his skill level was insufficient for his desired specialty. He could defensively dismiss this evaluation as just one tiny bit of feedback among many evaluations. Then Steve could devalue both its content and its source. Or he could defensively deflate his earlier goal, regarding surgery as nothing more than repetitive cutting and sewing, thinking of it as a specialty desired for him by his parents but not himself.

Altering the Threshold for Disengagement

Some patients in psychotherapy declare a topic concluded even though the therapist is quite sure that it has not been thoroughly contemplated. The problematic topic, with its emotional conflicts, is interrupted but not completed. A habitual tendency is one of moving or short-circuiting away from difficult decisions. If that happens, personal dilemmas remain unresolved and personal growth is retarded.

RECAPITULATION

Four control processes for affecting the contents of conscious experience are described in this chapter: altering topics, altering concepts, altering the importance of a chain of concepts to the self, and altering the threshold for disengaging awareness from a topic and its subcontents. These control processes affect an individual's awareness. They also affect communication and how ideas, feelings, intentions, and expectations are expressed in social actions and transactions.

Adaptive or maladaptive outcomes are the result of control processes. Some maladaptive outcomes are the result of relative failures of control; dreaded, undermodulated states are an example. Others are the result of excessive defensiveness. For purposes of clarification, Tables 4.1 and 4.2 give examples of adaptive and maladaptive defensive outcomes for each category of a defensive control process. However, it is important to note that most outcomes actually result from combinations of many control processes. The tables also show the effects when relative failure of regulation occurs.

Table 4.1 describes outcomes based on introspection and analysis of self-reported episodes of awareness in psychotherapy and on a questionnaire. Table 4.2 describes outcomes observers noted by reviewing a video, an audio, or a transcribed record of an interpersonal communication. These are outcomes psychotherapists might observe directly when discussing topics with a subject, and are the more reliable variables in clinical research.

The advantage of focusing on communicative signs, as in Table 4.2, is that the classification theory can be tested in research on psy-

TABLE 4.1
CONTENTS OF CONSCIOUS EXPERIENCE: OUTCOMES OF CONTROL PROCESSES

Control Processes	Defensive Outcomes		Failure of Regulation
	Adaptive	Maladaptive	
A. Altering Topics	Useful periods of contemplating and not contemplating a stressful topic (dosing); rational balances between internal and external sources of information	Topics of importance are not insightfully examined; needed decisions are not made; forgetting, disavowal, or denial of a stressful topic that requires resolution.	Intrusion of an emotionally overwhelming topic.
B. Altering Concepts	Useful contemplation of implications and possible solutions to problems; selective inattention to vexing or distressing concepts in order to gain restoration from distressing levels of emotion or loss of morale when problems seem insoluble; useful balancing of emotion by switching between concepts; establishment of a rational order of concepts.	Avoids key concepts; irrelevant details are amplified; moves from the emotional heart of a topic to its periphery in a way that leaves cause and effect sequences distorted or obscured	Disjointed or confused thought.
C. Altering the Importance to Self in a Chain of Concepts	Weighs alternatives and accepts the best solution to a problem amongst alternatives; accepts realistic estimates; appropriate humor.	Irrational exaggeration or minimization; excessive "sweet lemons" or "sour grapes" attitudes; rationalizes alternative solutions that are less rational than other solutions; inappropriate humor.	Sense of daze, emptiness, or chaotic shifts in attitudes.
D. Altering Threshold for Disengagement	Takes action when a good solution has been reached; accepts a new reality; makes efforts to practice new ways of thinking and acting, overrides outmoded unconscious ways of thinking and acting; tolerates high levels of negative emotion without derailing a topic, when processing that topic is beneficial.	Terminates contemplation of a topic prematurely; blocks reviews of memories or anticipation of threatening events; selects the emotionally easy but unrealistic choice; makes no choices on how to integrate contradictions.	Uncontrolled impulsive conclusions.

TABLE 4.2

CONTENTS OF INTERPERSONAL COMMUNICATIONS: OUTCOMES OF CONTROL PROCESSES

| Control Processes | Defensive Outcomes | | |
	Adaptive	Maladaptive	Failure of Regulation
A. Altering Topics	Expresses a potentially stressful topic to another person, to a degree that both can tolerate the emotion or conflict evoked with a balanced focus on self and other.	Unbalanced focus causing disruptive attention to self, or too attuned to other to be sufficiently attentive to topics of importance to self; does not present stressful topic(s); selects obscuring or misleading alternative topic(s).	Sudden plunges into and out of expressing emotionally overwhelming topics.
B. Altering Concepts	Communicates key facts and emotions; contemplates implications and possible solutions to problems; alert to cues of others.	Conceptual reluctance; misleads others who are potentially helpful; gives misinformation; generalizes when specifics are indicated; avoids expressing a concept that might prove useful in solving problems; switches facts back and forth; interrupts or overrides other to prevent clarification or a useful give and take; refuses to follow useful cues or leads provided by others.	Fragmented and hard to follow talk.
C. Altering the Importance to Self in a Chain of Concepts	Careful appraisal of alternatives; maintenance of clear changes in values, commitments, and shared meanings.	Vacillates when taking a stance is essential; facile face-saving at the expense of reasonable shared estimates of the truth; rationalizes the irrational.	Disruptive or chaotic shifts in attitudes.
D. Altering Threshold for Disengagement	Shares the decision-making process; makes decisions when in the best position to do so; selects the best topics and shows links between topics; accepts lead from others where that is best.	Avoids undesirable actions to prevent inner tensions; acts in an impairing manner to terminate a tense situation prematurely.	Uncontrolled impulsive talk or other actions.

73

chotherapy sessions using transcripts or tapes of interviews. Independent judges have followed systematic content analysis procedures and have applied definitions of defensive control to transcripts of psychotherapy sessions. Judges have rated different kinds of *elaboration* and *dyselaboration* of emotional ideas. The subcategories of dyselaboration have followed the Maladaptive column of Table 4.2. Judges scored text reliably by these categories. The category frequencies have shown increased use of dyselaboration during discourse on unresolved emotional topics (Horowitz, Milbrath, Reidbord, & Stinson, 1993; Horowitz, Milbrath, & Stinson, 1995).

CONTROLLING THE FORM OF CONSCIOUS EXPERIENCE

Emotion can be controlled by altering the forms of conscious experience. Five such processes include altering mode of representation, altering time span, altering logic level, altering level of action planning, and altering arousal level.

Altering Mode of Representation

People can shift the predominance of words, images, and somatic enactions in their conscious experience. People can have states in which there is relatively low translation of meanings between modes. Isolation of meaning in one mode, especially in the lexical mode, can reduce emotion. Increasing visual imagery can increase emotion.

If only visualization occurs, without translation into lexical meanings, awareness may be experienced as a passive activity without volitional effort, or as having an unintentional fantasy. Intense emotions can also occur and lead to a sense of loss of self-control. False memories, false fantasies, and occult experiences may even occur. That is why guided imagery states can be both evocative and risky.

Altering Time Span

Time spans include past, present, and future. Time spans can be boundaries and target areas for associational searches. Conscious attention may specifically focus on the remote and recent past, as well as the near and distant future. Contemplation can be limited by shifting attention away from a time when bad things did happen, or when they might happen in the future. For example, a person, on receiving news of laboratory tests that show cancer, might focus consciousness on only the present. This attentional shift helps the person deal with the immediate issues, such as planning possible treatment, and prevents the person from being swamped by emotions surrounding dreaded future risks. The person could also reduce emotion by focusing on the distant past, or relive a memory or fantasy in order to ignore current threats.

Altering Logic Level

People can change the rules they usually use to organize thought. Under stressful circumstances, they might shift from the tight logic of rational problem solving to loose, philosophical, even illogical associations. The opposite can also occur: People can blunt emotion by shifting from a broad logic of rational problem solving to one with a focus on minor details. When realistic planning threatens fear (for example, having to consider a likely future earthquake), people can reduce tension by preoccupying themselves with a creative fantasy about heroically rescuing all family members.

Altering Level of Action Planning

States of mind vary. In restful repose, the mental set is for contemplation without action. The set might even be to empty the mind to meditate without focusing on problem solving. On a basketball court, a different mental set is valuable, one favoring swift movement without distracting contemplation. Control processes can alter the ratio of reflective consciousness to motor activity. In playing ball games, action follows thought at lightning speed; in playing chess, action is restrained until thought is checked.

People can have varied outcomes from altering the set point. For example, they can affect their degree of thought and degree of concomitant motor activity. They can preoccupy themselves with one or the other to avoid unwanted emotional arousal: The preoccupation can be with rapid action such as playing a game of tennis, or with endless rumination of thought. The outcome can be adaptive if the preoccupation or absorption restores equilibrium in a time of strain. The outcome can be maladaptive if the person acts too impulsively instead of thinking, or excessively ruminates to avoid taking necessary action. Hamlet, for example, does both when he fails to act against his uncle, who murdered his father, and then impulsively stabs through a curtain, killing his mentor Polonious rather than his uncle.

Altering Arousal Level

People worry about energy, restlessness, or fatigue. They cannot always control their level of arousal. Yet control can be exerted by choosing calming or arousing activities, drugs, or stimuli. Both states of thrill and lethargy can reduce emotional threat. Joshing, bantering, giddiness, sexual promiscuity, and avoidant sleeping are sometimes used to avoid serious thought.

Table 4.3 summarizes the internal psychological outcomes (that is, the conscious experiences of several defensive control processes that control form); Table 4.4 summarizes the interpersonal outcomes.

CONTROLLING THE PERSON SCHEMAS THAT ORGANIZE A STATE OF MIND

Emotions can be changed by shifts in how a person views self and others. Five control processes can, in combination, change an internal working model of an actual social transaction: altering self schemas, altering schemas of other people, altering role-relationship models, altering value schemas, and altering executive agency schemas. These are described in the following sections, and outcomes are illustrated in Tables 4.5 and 4.6.

Altering Schemas of Self

Control of schemas of self can lead to shifts in roles. It can directly and indirectly alter the emotions that color a state of mind. A person usually has a repertoire of roles. By shifting roles within that repertoire, he or she can reduce the intensity of an unwanted emotion or the threat of an emotional conflict. This shift in identity can be recognized consciously, but it is usually motivated and carried out by unconscious processes. For example, Sophia may be thinking about trying out the artificial limb in physical therapy while priming a sense of herself as a tough fighter, a persevering and courageous woman, and the intelligent student of new tasks. This could lead to a *courageous* state of mind. Or she might think about the same topic

TABLE 4.3
FORM OF CONSCIOUS EXPERIENCE: OUTCOMES OF CONTROL PROCESSES

Control Processes	Defensive Outcomes		
	Adaptive	Maladaptive	Failure of Regulation
A. Altering Mode of Representation	Selective representation in all modes; lexical explanations; restorative imagery; somatic preparation.	Omission of useful modes; excessive numbing by avoiding images; avoids understanding images in words; prolonged escapist use of imagery or bodily enactions.	Intrusive and excessively vivid images (flashbacks), pseudo-hallucinations, hallucinations); enactive expression of raw emotions.
B. Altering Time Span	Looks at plans one step at a time to avoid being emotionally overwhelmed by long-term implications; relates an event to an entire life span to avoid being overwhelmed by long-term implications.	Denies urgency of a threat; disavows long-range implications to self; focuses on past or future to avoid need to make present decisions and take necessary actions.	Chaotic sense of time.
C. Altering Logic Level	Balance between rational planning and thought; restorative or creative fantasy.	Excessive preoccupation with small logical steps and details or with fantasy.	Confusion.
D. Altering Level of Action Planning	Restorative changes between activity and thought; prompt action at appropriate signs of opportunity; useful restraint.	Preoccupation with thinking to avoid important perceptions; preoccupation with perception to avoid necessary thinking; excessive action to avoid thought; excessive thought to avoid action; paralysis of action in favor of endless rumination.	Impulsive action and/or thought; no action.
E. Altering Arousal Level	Balance between arousal and rest cycles.	Excessive hypervigilance and compulsive worry or avoidant sleeping, reverie and lethargy.	Frenzied or exhausted states of mind.

TABLE 4.4

FORM OF INTERPERSONAL COMMUNICATIONS: OUTCOMES OF CONTROL PROCESSES

Control Processes	Defensive Outcomes		
	Adaptive	Maladaptive	Failure of Regulation
A. Altering Mode of Representation	Coherent mix of verbalization, facial signals, imagery metaphors, and bodily gestural movements.	Disruptive image metaphors; flat verbiage; discordant prosodics across words, voice, face, and body, leading to distortion, confusion, or a sense that something is warded off or being concealed.	Jumbles different expressive media; impulsive enaction of emotional signals.
B. Altering Time Span	Discusses coherent framing of time as to past, present, future, or imaginary perspectives.	Disruptive or confusing shifts in temporal perspective.	Chaotic timing of actions.
C. Altering Logic Level	Balance between rational planning (reflexive analyses) and restorative or creative fantasy (brainstorming); restorative humor or banter.	Disruptive or confusing shifts between analytic reasoning and fantasy; avoidant humor, joking, or banter.	Inability to follow a thread of meaning.
D. Altering Level of Action Planning	Appropriate and shared choices of when to talk and when to act; taking turns in a dialogue.	Avoidant disruption of turn-taking in a dialogue; acting out without recognition or sharing intentions in a dialogue; avoidant dialogue when acting is indicated; restless jittering to avoid thinking and feeling.	Impulsively excessive actions.
E. Altering Arousal Level	Appropriate lulls, silences, excitements, and turn-takings; useful cycles of activity and inactivity in complementary actions.	Excessive speed or slowing of actions to avoid useful confrontations.	Unavailable to shared communication because of excessive excitement or blunting.

TABLE 4.5

SCHEMAS THAT ORGANIZE CONSCIOUS EXPERIENCE: OUTCOMES OF CONTROL PROCESSES

Control Processes	Defensive Outcomes		
	Adaptive	Maladaptive	Failure of Regulation
A. Altering Self Schemas	Improved understanding of situation; enriched sense of identity.	Excessively grand or inferior beliefs about self; takes on a negative self schema to avoid identity diffusion; "subpersonalities".	Identity diffusion, states of depersonalization.
B. Altering Schema of Other Person	Enriched understanding of the intentions, motives, and predictable patterns of other.	Disregard of nature of other to preserve fantasy or personal stereotypes; changes the object of a feeling, wish, or source of threat from a more pertinent to a less pertinent one (displacement).	Impoverished understanding of other as a center of feelings and initiative.
C. Altering Role Relationship Models	Resilient change in internal working model of a current situation; useful learning through identification, mourning, resolving transferences.	Reverses roles inappropriate to the situation; switches working models into all-good or all-bad views of the relationship; changes the agent or source of an activity, wish, or feeling from self to other or other to self (role-reversal, projection).	Annihilation anxiety or panic on separations, states of derealization.
D. Altering Value Schemas (Critic Role)	Sagacious monitoring and judging of self and others, and of future critique of present choices; maintains useful vows and commitments; emancipatory self-reflections.	Unrealistic devaluation or idealization of self and/or other; switches values so rapidly that doubt paralyzes action.	Inability to evaluate moral consequences.
E. Altering Executive-Agency Schema	Restorative sense of being a part of something beyond self; intergenerational sense of responsibility for others.	Excessive surrender of best interests of self; excessive self-centeredness.	States of alienation.

TABLE 4.6

SCHEMAS THAT ORGANIZE INTERPERSONAL COMMUNICATIONS: OUTCOMES OF CONTROL PROCESSES

Control Processes	Defensive Outcomes		Failure of Regulation
	Adaptive	Maladaptive	
A. Altering Self Schema	Increase in competence and resilience within a situation; improved fit of behavior to the situation.	Jarring shift in "personality"; acting in a too-superior or too-inferior way; uses others as if they were part of, or extension of, the self.	Intentional signals are confusing.
B. Altering Schema of Other Person	Increase in understanding of the intentions, motives, and predictable patterns of other (empathy); ability to "read" another during an interaction.	Reacts to an internal misperception of the other; provokes the other to conform to an internal misperception (projective identification); short circuits to an inappropriate all-good or all-bad view of other; changes the object of a feeling, wish, or source of threat from the most pertinent one to a less pertinent one (displacement).	Chaotic views about what to expect from another in a situation.
C. Altering Role Relationship Models	Useful trials of a new pattern for a situation.	Disguises or undoes an intended script sequence by running an alternative, compromise, or opposite one (undoing, passive aggression); shimmering alternations of contradictory patterns; pretense of roles that are not felt authentically; preservation of an inappropriate script rather than acting flexibly as the situation unfolds; switches working models into all-good or all-bad views of the relationship; changes the agent or source of an activity, wish, or feeling from self to other, or other to self.	Inability to use relationships with others to stabilize a sense of identity.
D. Altering Value Schemas (Critic Role)	Points out the following of, or deflection from, values, rules, and commitments by self and others, in order to improve future situation.	Irrational assumptions of other's values to avoid social tension; inhibition of spontaneity by excessive monitoring; attributes blame irrationally outward to protect self-esteem.	Impulsive, punitive, revenge behaviors (on self or others).
E. Altering Executive-Agency Schema	Acts responsibly to care for others and to care for self as situations demand.	Unrealistic abnegation of self; suddenly selfish or autistic acts that disrupt relationships.	Inability to responsibly care for others.

while priming a sense of herself in the role of degraded, weak, incompetent, and abused little girl. This could lead to a *demoralized and deflated* state. The self schemas used to organize a chain of concepts will influence the associations that lead to elements in the chain.

Altering Schemas of Other

A person also has a repertoire of roles for others in general and various possible roles for a meaningful other in particular. Steve would have various roles for conceptualizing the senior surgeon, and each role might elevate or lower the surgeon's status with regard to Steve. Threatened by the statement from the senior surgeon that he had insufficient skills, Steve could not only devalue the memory of what was said, but devalue the role of the surgeon. Regarding the surgeon as a competent, high-status mentor would make the statements more threatening leading perhaps to an *anxious and shamed* state; altering the role for the surgeon into a personification of a martinet and snide judge who had feet of clay would minimize the shame that Steve tended to feel in response to the memory, perhaps leading to a state of cool *indifference*.

This example of Steve shows how the role of other might be altered from a high to a low status. The other, who is the target of contemplation, can also be shifted from one mental personification to another. That is, Steve could think of someone else, not the senior surgeon, and what this other person would say about his skills. People under stress often defensively displace the target of their emotion. If a strong boss makes a man feel fear, the man may get angry, but do nothing. However, he can take out his anger on a pet because it is weak and unlikely to retaliate. Many cartoons have shown the boss humiliating the employee, who is belligerent to a spouse, who spanks the child, who kicks the dog. Displacement is used to stifle the state of degradation felt by each person in the sequence.

Altering Role-Relationship Models

Role-relationship models are schemas of self and others that contain attributes and scripts of transaction. In any relationship, there may be different role-relationship models: Some may be desired, some feared, and some used as a compromise to avert dreaded states.

The outcome of the most common defensive control process follows: The person shifts to a state organized by a compromise role-relationship model. This occurs when a wish–fear dilemma links desired views to dreaded views of a relationship. The combination signals danger. The compromise avoids the threat posed by the dreaded consequences of the desired wish.

For example, a man may have a strong desire to have a loving relationship with an intelligent woman. He may fear that she is so knowledgeable that she will find him uninteresting. He wants to approach intimacy, but he fears rejection. He wants an *excited and close* state and fears a *lonely and dejected* state. A compromise state of mind can be organized by a role-relationship model in which he views himself as nonchalant, he can be in a *mildly amused* state, only moderately interested. The excitement of closeness and the pain of rejection are both reduced by his shift into the *mildly amused* compromise state. The defensive shift says, in effect, "Oh, I was just conversing to pass time until I go on to something else." The stance is "as if" rather than "real." The compromise eases the potential pain, but also reduces the potential joy.

People also shift role-relationship models in a way that reverses who feels what and who does what. For example, instead of thinking about fear, a person gets angry enough to project fear into someone else. Getting angry in order to escape from a dreaded state of fear entails taking on a stronger and more threatening position. This enables one to get away from his or her weaker and more vulnerable role. In one state, self may be viewed as a victim, and in another, as an aggressor. Now, self becomes the aggressor and the other, the victim.

Altering Value Schemas

All people engage in the conscious activity of judging the actions of others. People make critical analyses using alternative sets of values. At times some values conflict.

Different value schemas may be given different priorities in different states. When in danger of blame, as when shame threatens to destroy self-esteem, a person can control against such distress by shifting values. For example, a patient lied to his best friend in saying he was not dating the woman his friend was dating. This lie made him feel guilty because telling the truth is of value, as is the friendship. He shifted to the values of war, where deceit is part of a "good strategy." "Love is war," he said, and this shift in values reduced his guilt. Similar shifts become rationalizations in some businesses. A product with pollutants is sold because the business agent who is usually environmentally concerned is "just following orders," or is "loyal to the corporation."

Altering Executive Agency Schema

Executive agency refers to the person or persons believed to be in charge of forming plans and instigating action. In different states of mind, an individual may vary how his or her sense of executive agency affects decisions. In everyday life, the executive agent may be the "I." But in transition to another state, this executive agent may shift to something other than "I." Alternative agencies may be the "we" of a family or of intense friendships, the "we" of the work group, the "we" of homeland and folk, and the "they" that strongly influence the self's behavior. In dissociative conditions, there may be the alternative entity that does the good or bad deeds, thinks the positive or negative thoughts. Beyond the "they" of "should," there are also the "they" of "they made me do it" and the demons of demonic possession.

Sometimes seeing "I" as an executive agent feels too impoverished and one's mood deflates. The small lonely self inflates by shifting executive agency to a larger force or group. A sense of merger with cosmic powers can occur, with adaptive or maladaptive consequences. Morale may be restored as grander agents are in charge, but grandiose delusions may also be formed. Illusions of powerful connections buoy feelings but lead to irrational attitudes.

RESEARCH BASE

As previously mentioned, the classification of control processes and outcomes presented in Tables 4.1 through 4.6 evolved from clinical research. The empirical work began with intensive case studies of patients in psychotherapy for stress-response syndromes (Horowitz, 1973, 1974, 1997; Horowitz, Fridhandler, & Stinson, 1991; Horowitz, Markman, Stinson, et al., 1990; Horowitz, Znoj, & Stinson, 1996). It included quantitative investigation of the reliability and validity of categories of the defensive outcomes shown in the tables. These variables included dyselaborations, disavowals, (Horowitz, Milbrath, Reidbord, and Stinson, 1993), nonverbal warding-off behaviors (Horowitz, Stinson, Curtis, et al., 1993), and shifting into overmodulated states to stifle emotion (Horowitz, Stinson, Curtis, et al., 1993;

Horowitz, Milbrath, Ewent, Sonneborn and Stinson, 1994; Horowitz, Milbrath, Jordan, et al., 1994). Reliably scored signs of such defensive control efforts were found to locate the most emotional and conflictual topics in psychotherapy (Horowitz, Milbrath, & Stinson, 1995).

Defensive role-relationship models were also studied. These were reliably rated by independent judges (Horowitz & Eells, 1993) and independent formulation teams, blind to each others' inferences; they were able to arrive at similar defensive configurations for the same case material (Eells, et al., 1995; Horowitz, Eells, Singer, & Salovey, 1995).

Additional empirical checks on the theory of classification of defensive control processes shown in the tables were then conducted. The research included separate studies of observers who viewed recorded videotapes, and subjects in both normal and emotionally perturbed populations who rated their own defenses. People reported on their own control processes with good test–retest reliability, independent judges agreed reliably in scoring recorded segments of interviews (Hans Znoj and Mardi Horowitz, unpublished research communication, 1998). Observers concurred reliably. Clinicians have found the categories presented in the table useful in formulating their own cases (Horowitz, 1997b, Horowitz, Cooper, Fridhandler, et al., 1992).

SUMMARY

People regulate awareness to stabilize emotion and avoid dreaded states of mind. This chapter examines different types of control processes to achieve this purpose. Three filigreed sets for alterations in active contents, forms, and personal schemas are presented. Tables illustrate various possible outcomes for each type of control. However, every outcome is really the result of combinations of simultaneous and transactive use of several types of control.

Control processes and outcomes vary in different states; shifts in control processes may be an important reason why a person shifts from one state to another. Observing such shifts is helpful for inferring what is not being thought or said.

Conscious choices to focus attention on a particular topic can sometimes override nonconscious controls. These choices can operate against nonconscious control processes and modify awareness. Nonconscious controls that favored avoidance in the past become unnecessary in the present. Conscious choices can now approach difficult-to-solve conflictual themes.

CHAPTER 5

Identity

IDENTITY IS motivational in that people want self-respect and work hard to reduce self-loathing. Because of its immense importance, most schools of psychology have addressed this topic. But agreed on theory has been difficult to achieve. One reason lies in the complexity of a key observation: Self concepts can vary across the person's different states of mind. A theory of multiple self schemas is necessary to explain this observation. The more a person can organize these multiple self schemas into a coherent whole, the more likely that individual is to experience a sense of identity cohesiveness and continuity over extended periods of time.

Most psychologists define the sense of identity as a conscious experience of the self as one who perceives, thinks, feels, and exists over time. Locke (1690) centered on a key property: a sense of sameness over time (Erikson, 1959; Lichtenstein, 1977). According to the central thesis of this chapter—multiple available schemas of self—this sense of sameness is sometimes illusory. But also according to the theory to be presented, the sense of sameness is realistic and not illusory; it is derived from supraordinate configurations that can associate multiple self schemas. People can change by forming supraordinate integrations; they can progress from a scattered sense of vagrant identity to an abiding harmony.

SELF SCHEMAS

A self schema is an organized compendium of meanings that a person attributes to his or her self. It is a patterned aggregation of elements, not a random multiplicity of attributes. A self schema is an ordered constellation of associated beliefs (Jacobson, 1964; Schilder, 1950; Singer & Salovey, 1991). The connected and associated beliefs of a particular self schema make up a structure of nonconscious knowledge, which can be realistic or unrealistic in both contents and linkages between contents.

Repertoires of unconscious self schematized knowledge exist, with more or less active units. Activated self schemas influence working models. Working models combine with perceptions to organize representations into conscious experiences. Self-observation of self-experiencing, in reflective consciousness, then leads to a sense of current identity. This experience can match or mismatch with memory of a prior sense of identity.

Conscious experiences include concepts about the self in the past, present, and future. In various states, a person can hold different views of past identity. Less surprising, he or she can also imagine various future selves. Some futures are idealized, others realistic; some are desired, others dreaded. Moreover, in shimmering states of mind, contrasting self-concepts can be consciously experienced. This is often due to the organizing activity of two or more self schemas.

Self schemas are a pattern of nonconscious associations between various units of belief about self-attributes. These schematized attributes could be potential declarative knowledge, such as "I am a saintly mother." In other instances, procedural knowledge is schematized, leading to particular styles of expressing, gesturing, and moving. The procedural knowledge could lead to enactive representations such as a saintly posturing of the face, hands, and body.

One of many categories of meaning in a self schema is a cognitive map of the physical self and its somatic usage. The somatic styles of an individual often vary in different moods; this can be observed in the systematic variance in walk, gesture, voice, and facial expression. Observers can infer another person's self schemas from such observations and by listening to reports of his or her consciously visualized or kinesthetically felt body sensations. Observers can then describe that person's body images as part of his or her self schemas.

Another category of beliefs within self schemas includes the roles and intentions of self. Roles of self are often embedded in expectations about roles for other people. Scripts for how the self can, or does, react to others are included in such role-relationship models. Scripts of action sequences are associated with roles and body images. Values, rules, and self-regulatory styles are also categories in a self schema. All these elements in the associations of beliefs that form a self schema are summarized here:

- Body image
- Roles of self
- Associated memories of self;
- Emotional response style;
- Scripts of action sequences;
- Values and rules;
- Self regulatory style; and
- Future intentions and plans.

These are all mental contents that might differ from one self schema to another. In addition, linkages between contents, such as a body image and a role, could differ from one self schema to another.

People vary in their degree of development of a complex sense of identity. At the level of self schemas, complexity and differentiation are a matter of how well the person has combined smaller networks of associations into larger systems of meanings that are self-related. In other words, people differ in the degree to which they have integrated several self schemas into a supraordinate schema.

A *supraordinate schema* is a schema of many schemas, a higher system combining lower systems of associated beliefs. Figure 5.1 shows linking across self schemas to form supraordinate self-knowledge. People who have more supraordinate self schemas can have a more integrated self-organization. But conflicted components within the supraordinate schema can limit that integration.

In any particular state of mind, a person could derive his or her conscious sense of identity from information in just one self schema. Another experience of identity could be formed from a supraordinate schema combining several possible selves. If these possible selves are not conflicted, the result can be a richer and more differentiated episode of self-reflection.

Figure 5.1 depicts a theory about a hierarchy of self schematization. This theory indicates how people may vary in level of supraordinate schematization. Some people have developed only singular self schemas, and these may even be dissociated from one another. Others have formed supraordinate schemas. These reduce the likelihood of dissociation, even under stress. Some people have many con-

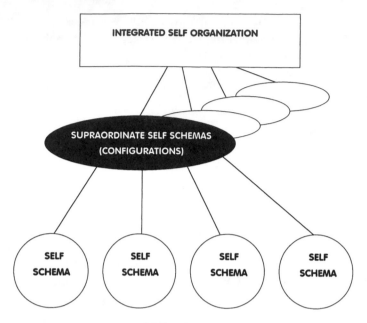

FIGURE 5.1
Hierarchical Nesting of Self Schemas

tradictions across schemas, even within a supraordinate network of personal meanings. They may be mature but still quite conflicted. Other people have less antithetical alternative roles for self. Their characterological maturity is likely to seem more mellow and harmonious.

This assertion deserves repetition in its negative form. People with few supraordinate schemas, and with antithetical self schemas, are vulnerable to explosive shifts in state. Under stress they are vulnerable and in conscious memory are apt to dissociate their various identity experiences. They tend to use defensive control processes that disavow or distort reality instead of those that lead to a dose-by-dose style of coping with emotional challenges.

Further explanations are presented here in the context of two simplified, fictional examples, derived from composites of many clinical observations.

MATTHEW AND BILL

Matthew and Bill were brothers who had an accident while riding in their truck together. They both had serious physical consequences.

Their responses to illness varied because of their different pre-accident self schemas.

Before the accident, Matthew often entered a worried state in which he feared that a minor pain meant he had a serious disease. An unusual heartbeat, gas pain, or weight loss of 2 pounds might send him to his physician for reassurance. His repetitive *hypochondriacal misery* state was based, in part, on a self schema as being fragile and vulnerable to physical damage. This self schema developed in part because of his genetic endowment and early biology: He was smaller and thinner than others in his family. It also developed, in part, because he played a sickly role.

Matthew had another self schema; when it organized a state of *proud entitlement*, he played the role of an aristocrat, one allowed to break usual rules to gain personal satisfactions that were his due. In states organized by this self schema, Matthew, as a child, would take long hot baths rather than doing his assigned chores. He would grandly help himself to many desserts instead of eating any of the more nutritious dishes. His parents chided him for his attitude and predicted a dire future: He would make himself sick. Yet they sympathized with him when he was in his *hypochondriacal misery* state, so they were inconsistent.

These factors in his environment contributed to a cycle in which Matthew would shift from a state of *proud entitlement*, organized by a grandiose self schema, to a fearful state of *hypochondriasis*, organized by his fragile self schema. But once in a *hypochondrical misery* state, Matthew would shift again. Instead, he felt a state of *pleasant receptivity* toward expected sympathy. His hope, now that he had paid the price for being bad was that he would regain personal goodness and good care from others. He cycled from self-indulgence, to suffering, to redemptive recovery, and back to self-indulgence; his states cycled from *proud entitlement*, to *hypochondrical misery*, to *pleasant receptivity*, to *proud entitlement*.

Bill was older, larger, and much more muscular than Matthew. Bill was a robust child and developed a strong, competent, and invulnerable self schema. Whereas Matthew expected to lose his health in the future because of excessive self-indulgences (which he nonetheless repeated), Bill never expected to be ill. At times he had a fantasy of dying gallantly like a heroic knight for the great cause of saving his loved ones. They would then idealize him. In his fantasy of martyrdom he did not expect terminal suffering and extended non-being; the realities of death were not part of his script.

In adulthood, Bill acted the martyr role by doing most of the work when he was in partnership with Matthew. Bill's parents had always praised him as the hard-working boy and criticized Matthew as the slacker. Bill expected good things as the result of his high levels of work, and he expected bad things to happen if he slacked off. He also had a dreaded self schema of being a dirty, selfish, nasty boy. He hated being seen as a bully just because he was strong and willful. Bill's martyr role prevented his fear of greedily hurting others from being realized.

Bill and Matthew were in a partnership in which they worked together as truck drivers, taking turns at the wheel so that they could cover long distances. On an icy mountain pass, their tanker truck skidded into a ditch and overturned. A rupture in one of the pipes released a cloud of toxic gas that resulted in lung damage to both brothers. After a lengthy hospitalization, they faced a long convalescence.

As Matthew and Bill slowly recovered, each had episodes of fright when they found it difficult to breathe. During this illness, Matthew showed a greater ability than Bill to cooperate with the pulmonary treatment program, and more stamina in enduring discomforts and frights. This surprised everyone in the family, who had expected the opposite because of Matthew's periodic hypochondriasis and role as an invalid.

Many factors seemed to account for the role reversal; perhaps foremost among them was the fact that Matthew had already rehearsed how to be a patient. Scripts for how to act within a role are aspects of self schemas. His script did not include death as an outcome. His usually unconscious script of how and why one has an illness contained the belief that the illness was retribution, that it would cleanse him of previous contaminations from his past self-centered actions. When this long-feared infirmity occurred, it was a relief, a penance long overdue. He met his illness with hope, based on an expectation of a favorable outcome. Moreover, he believed health care professionals were typically caring, competent, and helpful, like his parents; they would be sympathetic about his illness. He spent his time in the hospital often in a state of *pleasant receptivity*.

Bill, in contrast, had unconscious beliefs in self as invulnerable. He believed that if any illness or death struck a family member, it would strike Matthew. He never expected personal incapacity and had not rehearsed that role. He believed that only weak people had disabilities. He did not have a script for how to behave as a patient and did not view health professionals as helpers. He was unable to work; he felt dirty and greedy taking help from others, and he expected to be criticized as a slacker. He spent his time in the hospital in mixed states of anxiety, tension, fear, shame, and self disgust.

The abrupt change to a realistic fear of dying during states of difficult breathing also terrified him. He had a recurrent fantasy of being buried alive and would enter into an undermodulated state of fear. Bill expected dire events, whereas Matthew expected redemption.

In the cases of Matthew and Bill, disabilities following the accident led to shifts in dominant self schemas, and so to shifts in states of mind.

JOHN AND SUE

John and Sue had not yet met, but each had a similar pattern of falling in and out of love frequently. Both longed for a deeper and more enduring relationship than either had yet experienced. In this fictional example, John and Sue are depicted as having the same types of desired, dreaded, and more realistic self-appraisals. The similar self-appraisals resulted from identity experiences organized by multiple self schemas and are simplified as follows:

Desired self-appraisal.   I am exceptionally talented and physically attractive.
Realistic self-appraisal.   I am relatively attractive and interesting.
Dreaded self-appraisal.   I am ugly and boring.

When desired self-appraisals occurred, John or Sue entered a *desired vivacious and excited* state of mind. When dreaded selves become dominant, an unwanted state of *disgust and withdrawal* occurred. When the realistic self was dominant, each entered into a state that was *open and receptive*.

At a large party, John and Sue flirted and saw each other as vivacious and attractive. They kindled mutual interest; each felt enhanced by the other. Both felt vivacious and excited; they decided to date. Idealizations of each other fueled romantic love; together they felt exceptional. Ideal self concepts occurred in the reflective consciousness of each partner.

As John and Sue spent time together, they were no longer always at their best. Sue learned that John was sometimes clumsy and morose. At the same time, John observed that Sue was sometimes irritable and withdrawn. Zest and excitement disappeared for a time.

Each partner had states when they appraised themselves as ugly and boring. Interchanges with each other became flat. Each blamed the other for "losing the magic" in their relationship.

Both had frequent states of disgust and withdrawal. Each decided to turn to another person in the hopes of regaining lost liveliness in a new flirtation. With the new companions, they both again entered into vivacious and excited states. Self-appraisals as sometimes ugly and boring gave way to more frequent self-appraisals as exceptionally talented and attractive. The others were exhilarating companions. This return of zest convinced each of them, separately, of their rightness in deciding to turn away from the other. John told people that he had the insight that Sue was "somehow bad for him" and she did the same.

John and Sue repeated the pattern with their new companions. Each again felt dejected and lonely, and each decided to seek the other out again. In continuing their special friendship, they developed more comprehensive views. They developed *supraordinate schemas* that allowed them to anticipate ebbs and flows of excitement. Each learned how to help the other through a bad mood of disgust and withdrawal; when one felt ugly and boring, the other decided to be empathic, soothing, and restoring rather than to withdraw. They learned compassion and support. They each forged working models and schemas that associatively linked good and bad memories of their relationship. This complex network of linkages deepened their attachment. They were able to smooth and soften occasional shifts into dreaded states. Each had heightened awareness of self and other as a couple with ups and downs.

In this imaginary scenario, Sue and John went through alterations of self schemas within a repertoire. They developed supraordinate schemas and a capacity for staying together through the high and low points of a committed relationship.

SCRIPTS AND FUTURE INTENTIONS IN SELF SCHEMAS

Self schemas, often embedded in role relationships with others, include transactional sequences called *scripts* (Abrams, 1994; Berne,

1961; Turner, Hogg, Oakes, & Reicher 1987). Some of these scripts involve intentions and even specific future plans. These plans help to appraise a current situation, and help examine it in terms of contingencies for possible action. Some scripts and future plans are learned by mimicry of others. Within one's imagination, many revisions of scripts can then take place. The following vignettes illustrate some aspects of such scripts.

Tom

Tom, age 15, watched his older brother, age 17, court a young woman. The couple engaged in various sexual overtures. His brother had spoken crudely about previous sexual acts, which had led Tom to have raw, lust-filled fantasies. Now Tom was surprised by his brother's courtliness, courtesy, and loving fondness. Tom had formerly conceived a schema of prudish female reserve and brutal male lovemaking. After observing his brother's current behavior, Tom revised his former script and developed a new script for the future.

Herman

Scripts and plans for the future can include pathogenic elements (Weiss & Sampson, 1986). Herman, a preschooler, had a sister who was 1 year younger. With his 5-year-old mind, it seemed to Herman that their mother loved the sister more. He envied her; he planned how to squeeze her out and get more love for himself. One day, while they were playing together in the street, he saw her get hit by a car; she was killed instantly. Many adaptations had to be made due to this terrible experience. One was that Herman had to change his plan for gaining love and attention.

Herman felt guilty because he associated his former plan to squeeze out his sister with her death. He then unconsciously evolved a more complex fantasy; he would gain love and then lose it. By losing it, he could atone for his envy and his wish to replace his sister. He could reduce guilt from the childlike belief that his resentment had caused her traumatic death.

As a grown man, Herman unconsciously repeated a maladaptive pattern based on this fantasy; he loved and lost repeatedly and unnecessarily. He even threatened to leave treatment and the therapist who was trying to help him resolve this neurotic repetition. The therapist interpreted this threat as a transference enactment and a repetition of the same pattern. Together, Herman and the therapist clarified the substrates of this pattern. Herman gained insight and learned to tolerate his emotional horror surrounding his sister's death. He modified his script for the future, intending to love and retain affection rather than compelling himself to lose important affiliations.

CONFLICTUAL CONFIGURATIONS

Within an integrative cognitive map, a person's varied roles can blend smoothly with each other. When this happens, the person can use the supraordinate system to promote a seamless, resilient, and situationally appropriate shifting of states. However, roles within a configuration can also contradict each other. A supraordinate schema is *integrated* if the larger system contains beliefs about how to balance the antithesis; it is *conflicted* if it contains enduring but poorly integrated connections between elements. Maladaptive state cycles are associated with conflicted and nonintegrated supraordinate configurations.

Conflicted supraordinate configurations contain dilemmas of purpose: The person may anticipate both desired and dreaded outcomes of the same aims. The threatening and dreaded consequences of wishes can be prevented through a shift into schemas for defensive compromises. Then neither the wished-for role nor the feared role is activated. Instead, the person activates the defensive self schema, which reduces risk of entering into an out-of-control and dangerous state of mind. The conflicted configuration includes the desired, dreaded, and compromise roles.

Conflictual configurations contain antithetical or contradictory beliefs that are associated despite the discord. A wish–fear dilemma about being strong is an example: The person may desire to be the strongest one of all, yet also dread being seen as too strong, a threatening rival to be destroyed or a cruel victor who is excessively harmful to others. The desired state might be gloriously victorious, but the dreaded states contain potentials for intense fears of revenge or suicidal levels of guilt. A harmonious configuration would contain less discordant and antithetical beliefs. For example, the person may desire to be strong and fear an unfair use of personal power at the expense of others. The desired state is joy of winning and the dreaded state is remorse over diminishing the status of a rival. This positive–negative polarity is less extreme than that of the conflictual configuration. The harmonious configuration permits acceptable blends of competition and cooperation, as in the controlled rivalries of department heads in a corporation.

The fictional case of Tom illustrates in more detail a conflictual supraordinate configuration of self schemas.

TOM

Tom, age 25, wanted to feel strong in social roles, but he feared feeling too strong. If he felt too strong, he shifted to weaker roles to undo the threat. Likewise, if he felt too weak, he shifted to stronger roles to avoid the threat of succumbing to another person. These personality patterns put Tom in conflict when he requested a big favor from his friend Bill. Tom asked Bill for the loan of a large sum of money, and Bill refused him. Before Bill's refusal, Tom was in a state organized by a role for self as an assertive, worthwhile friend. This was a state of well-modulated *engagement*. After Bill's refusal, Tom could respond with anger from his role as an assertive, worthwhile friend. He could remain engaged and well-modulated, telling Bill why Bill should reconsider his negative decision. Tom could express himself in a firm but nonthreatening way

An alternative reaction to Bill's rebuff would be for Tom to shift his state to a role of righteous avenger with a script for angry shouting, entering a dreaded undermodulated state of *rage*. Yet another alternative would be to shift into a problematic compromise state of *haughter* with shimmering emotions: both restraint and a stifling of rage. Tom could show Bill arrogance, disdain, and restrained hostility, stemming from a personal role as an insulted aristocrat. Another defensive alternative would be entry into an overmodulated quasi-adaptive compromise state, one of being *aloof*, organized by a self-schema as an independent loner who no longer wants a false friend.

Four alternative self-stances have been mentioned in this chapter, and all could be associated into a supraordinate configuration of Tom's strong self schemas. Tom's configuration contained a desired role as worthwhile friend, a dreaded role as righteous avenger, and defensive roles as insulted aristocrat and independent loner. These self schemas could organize his potential anger at the rebuff into different experiences, in well-modulated, undermodulated, shimmering, or overmodulated states, as shown in Figure 5.2.

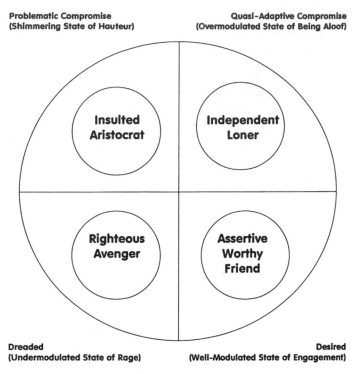

Problematic Compromise
(Shimmering State of Hauteur)

Quasi-Adaptive Compromise
(Overmodulated State of Being Aloof)

Insulted
Aristocrat

Independent
Loner

Righteous
Avenger

Assertive
Worthy
Friend

Dreaded
(Undermodulated State of Rage)

Desired
(Well-Modulated State of Engagement)

FIGURE 5.2
TOM'S STRONG SELF SCHEMAS

Another set of states might occur if Tom activated a configuration of weak roles for self. Such a configuration is depicted in Figure 5.3. He might repeat his request, in a humbler way, in a well-modulated state of *supplication* organized by a self schema as a likable, financially weaker friend. Alternatively, on being rebuffed, Tom might switch to feeling like a disgusting, greedy little boy who had asked for an excessive favor and been rightfully scorned. This latter alternative would be a shift into a dreaded and undermodulated state of *shame.* Tom could avoid that *shame* state by shifting self schemas to that of a timid little boy who with uncertainty and tension tried to both get closer and remain distant from his friend, in a shimmering state of *approach and withdrawal.* Another alternative: Tom could enter an overmodulated state of *banter* to avoid shame. He could switch to a self-schema of buffoon, taking distance from his own request while disengaging from its inappropriate quality by showing that he was just joking.

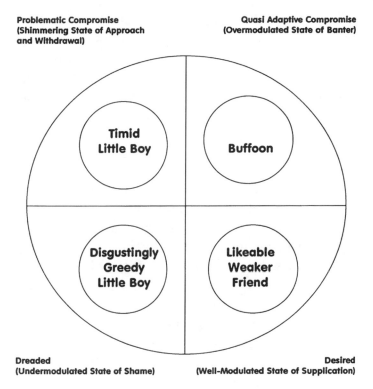

FIGURE 5.3
Tom's Weak Self Schemas

This fictional vignette illustrates two configurations, each with four alternative self schemas, leading to eight possible states for Tom as a reaction to Bill's rebuff. Tom's personality contains this repertoire for eight states.

Tom is a fictional case to illustrate personality complexity at the level of self schemas. An actual case, that of Bella, illustrates how a complex pattern can be deciphered from the analysis of a series of social transactions. Self schemas and role-relationship models and their scripts, can be recognized by observing repeated patterns. Bella also illustrates configurations of dreaded, desired, problematic compromise, and quasi-adaptive compromise self schemas. Moreover, this example shows how shifting self schemas can lead to mercurial fluctuations in states, as well as how configurations of states and self schemas can be brought into awareness, lead to insight, and to decisions that reduce the frequency of explosive or self-impairing shifts.

BELLA

Bella, a 35-year-old computer programmer, organized complex systems in a major corporation. She had unique skills but was turned down for promotion. One day, she arrived at work intoxicated. She was then referred for treatment by the medical director. She was told that she could continue work if she sought treatment; she did so grudgingly.

Initial exploratory psychotherapy sessions kindled her interest. In exploring why she had done something so unusual as to drink before work, she said, "It serves those weak-minded bosses right; I can out-perform anyone at work in any condition." The therapist said that this sounded like magical thinking. She was surprised and captivated by the therapist's remark.

In a subsequent session, she told of more episodes that involved choices based on magical thinking. At work, she launched projects prematurely because she wanted sudden accomplishments. At home, she aimed at improving her condominium with carpentry projects. She sometimes plunged rapidly ahead without planning. For example, before sawing, she did not measure the wood; she used eyeball estimates for critical lengths. The phrase *magical thinking* intrigued her because, although she knew better, she liked to believe that she could act with amazing speed and accomplish a project perfectly.

As the therapy explored Bella's varied states of mind, it became clear that a *sour* state of agitated despondancy and bitter resentment preceded magical thinking. Bella used magical thinking when she needed a way to enter a *thrilled* state to relieve her mood. Magical thinking, she said, produced more thrills than alcohol. In her magical thoughts she achieved great recognition for her talents. But, if she imagined she failed, she shifted back to the *sour* state. These states had themes connected to a wish fear dilemma.

Bella switched topics as a defensive control. She said very little about her experiences of self during the *sour* state. When the therapist directed her attention back to the topic of this *sour* state, being alienated from and neglected by others, she shifted into a new state, one of contemptuous disdain in which she mocked the therapist. She said that he was just another mental health jerk. This was her *carping* state of mind; it oscillated during sessions, with *sour* states, which involved self-disgust rather than contempt for the therapist.

In her *sour* state, as shown in Figure 5.4, Bella identified herself as disgustingly full of hate, like a little, ugly wretch, seething with rage. She called herself a "hate baby." This dreaded identity of hate baby disappeared under the influence of alcohol or with thrills during rapid-fire projects. Magical thinking kept the thrill going: A fantasy of herself as a wonder-worker whose pride over a great product displaced any self-disgust. When the magic failed, she shifted to a role of "superior critic of others," entering her *carping* state. This role defended against her loss of self-esteem. Any failure of her own was still insignificant compared to the dumb efforts of others, as she expressed in her opening remark about weak-minded bosses.

Her *thrilled* state, with a self-concept as a wonder woman, and her *carping* state, with a self-concept as a superior critic, kept her above others. She desired the identity of wonder woman and used the superior critic role as a compromise. It prevented her from entering a dreaded *sour* state with disgusting self-concepts as hate baby.

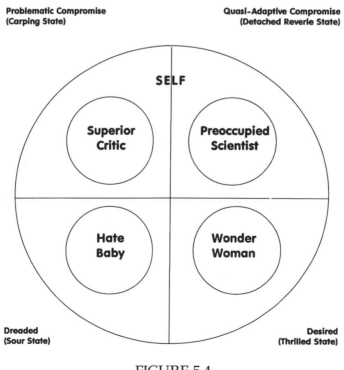

FIGURE 5.4
BELLA'S SELF SCHEMAS

Bella used various defensive control processes besides switching topics to avoid her *sour* state. She altered meanings to magnify maladroit behaviors of others and to minimize the effects of her own self-impairing and irrational actions. In evaluating the cause and effect of a messy situation, she would slide meanings and shift values to make other people look bad. The meaning was distorted as she slid blame away from herself and externalized it to others.

Bolstered by altered critical schemas of repeated experiences of emotionally safe transactions with the therapist, Bella became able to accept clarifications and interpretations without entering a *carping* state. A new state emerged during therapy: *detached reverie*. She would utter a phrase or two indicative of insight, but then would fall into a long silence. Her body posture and gestures seemed out of touch.

When the therapist asked for her thoughts, Bella flared up and criticized him for interfering. She then realized this was like the situation at work where she regularly became upset when interrupted. She felt like a preoccupied scientist interrupted by pea brains. Whenever colleagues communicated with her, she would enter a *carping* state and criticize them. This pattern of snapping waspishly at others was the reason she was passed over for promotion. She continued to be accepted at her job because of her creative brilliance, but her sharp, peevish behavior made her impossible to work with.

A number of states were observed and discussed in Bella's treatment: Two had strong negative emotions, the *carping* and *sour* states; one was relatively less negative, the *detached reverie*; and one contained positive emotions, the *thrilled* state. These states frequently occurred in a state cycle. The cycle was emotionally motivated by beliefs about the self during each state. Bella desired the positive emotion of the *thrilled* state and her self schema as wonder woman. But working of wonders was sometimes based on magical rather than realistic expectations. Real events prevented the realization of her wishes, such as when a miscut board did not fit into its assigned place and disrupted a carpentry project, or when a sequence in a computer program produced a bug rather than a butterfly. When her attempts at stabilizing a *thrilled* state as a wonder working woman failed, her state shifted, and she plummeted into the abyss of her *sour* state, filled with self-disgust.

This *sour* state was dreaded but repeated. Bella would escape the dreaded *sour* state by entering the *carping* state, where she would rationalize criticism and deflect rage onto others. This was the recurrent problem that had put her job in jeopardy, but it did have its upside: She could feel superior rather than feel like a baby, and she could judge others. Nonetheless, this problematic compromise could be improved. She shifted into a *detached reverie*, as if contemplating the weighty problems under criticism. She was now in the role of preoccupied scientist, not bothered by others. This was a quasi-adaptive position for Bella; it disengaged her from issues of blaming either herself or others for frustrations. When ready, she could once again shift and enter the *thrilled* state.

Magical thinking was important because it created a dilemma: On the one hand, it lifted her spirits, but on the other hand, it was unrealistic. Her actions based on deflections from reality caused her failure and dashed her spirits. Therapy helped Bella gain conscious control through use of awareness and insight to reach new decisions. She was able to see the pattern of the state cycle, and her various hoped-for and feared identity experiences in each state. She was able to gradually reduce her use of magical thinking and to soften her self-disgust through real accomplishments and the praise she began to receive for her excellent work.

MOTIVATION AND SELF SCHEMAS

The cases of Tom and Bella illustrate multiple selves. They clarify a theoretical conceptualization and compartmentalize certain self-views. This approach is helpful for teaching and is often useful in psychotherapy.

A HISTORICAL PERSPECTIVE

The role of self schemas in motivation has been a matter of debate. At one extreme, goals of self-preservation and identity enhancement are declared to be core intentions. At the other extreme, goals of self as consciously experienced are illusions produced by deeper motives. Competing theories of motivation and units of personification of self have seldom been resolved into a general agreement.

Multiple and split off selves became a topic of interest in the 19th century, partially because of the discovery of hypnosis (Ellenberger, 1970).

James (1890, 1910) criticized theories about multiple unconscious selves that emerged, and emphasized only conscious experiences. Freud (1903) emphasized unconscious psychodynamics. He posited unconscious sets of conflicting motives for self as ego, id as an it-like biological force, and an over-self called the superego. But Freud did not explore the source of identity-formation as a basic motive. Jung (1939), Klaif (1984), Whitmont (1969) did then focus upon this topic. Janet (1925) and Pittman, et al., (1990), Van der Kolk (1994) focused attention on multiple states with varied identity experiences that were dissociated. Erikson (1958) brought a multiple-selves perspective into Freudian theory, as did M. Klein (1948), Winnicott (1955, 1958), Jacobson (1964), Kernberg (1967, 1982, 1992), and Kohut (1972). Kohut (1977) rejected psychosexual motivation in self-development and evolved motivation as a striving for coherence and empathic recognition of identity. Klein (1976) and Gill (1976) grew dissatisfied with the id/ego/superego theoretical scaffolding. Their theories pointed to self-organization as part of a fundamental motivation for coherence and emotional control. A similar view developed simultaneously in British object relations psychology (Bowlby, 1969; Fairbairn, 1954; Guntrip, 1971; M. Klein, 1948; Winnicott, 1958).

A group of academic scholars with a strong psychoanalytic orientation embarked on a very relevant empirical study of personality. Henry Murray led this group at Harvard University in the 1930s. His categories of needs and presses were initially conceptualized as derivatives of sexual and aggressive drives of the id. The group expectation was that recurrent patterns of specific needs and presses would characterize individuals who were tested in diverse ways by scientists. The results were expected to support instinctual drive typologies, but they failed to do so. Instead, self- and relational theories were supported. That is, the group found that the individual characteristics of the subjects studied were best defined by relational patterns between self and others: These characteristics were called *themas* (Murray, 1938). The themas appeared as repeated patterns in expressions, and would be based on what are called *person schemas* in this book. Similar results, patterns of recurrent self–other themas as motivational, followed in academic psychology research on personal constructs (Apter, 1989; Kelly, 1955; Neimeyer, 1986).

As cognitive science emerged, quantitative methods for study of self evolved (Kihlstrom, 1987; Kihlstrom & Cantor, 1994; Kreitler & Kreitler, 1982; Linville & Carlston, 1994; Markus, 1977; Zajonc, 1980). A theme of agreement was found: multiple possible selves. This work empirically confirmed theories of the constructivist structuralist psychologists (Bartlett, 1932; Bower & Gilligan, 1979; Markus, 1977; Piaget, 1930; Rogers, Kuiper, & Kirker, 1977). Theories from cognitive science blended surprisingly well with psychodynamic theories (Higgins, 1987; Horowitz, 1977a, 1977b, 1988a, c, 1991a; Kreitler & Kreitler, 1982; Linville & Carlston, 1994; Singer & Salovey, 1991; Stein, 1981; Wylie, 1974).

By conceptualizing a possible unitary self-organization that can link together multiple alternative self schemas, the debate between singular self-agency and multiplicity partially disappears. Self schemas then group together into supraordinate forms when associated with particular kinds of relationships with others. With a mother, one may have desired, dreaded and compromise self concepts. Those might influence subsequent relationships with women who care for the self. Systematic differences and similarities in self conceptualization, in different contexts, has been examined in research on clinical case formulations (Horowitz, 1979b, 1991a, 1997a, b; Horowitz, Eels, Singer, & Salovey, 1995; Ryle, 1975; Strupp & Binder, 1984). In normal populations, Kihlstrom and Cantor (1994) found different configurations of selves with different relationships: Self schemas of being with a mother were different from self schemas associated with ties to a father. Theoretical and research studies have also shown how several self schemas may unite by association and produce a supraordinate configuration (Hart, Stinson, Field, Ewert, & Horowitz, 1995; Horowitz & Zilberg, 1983; Kihlstrom & Cantor, 1994). Some configurations may be specific to certain types of relationships, such as leader–follower, husband–wife and parent–child. These configurations help a person to express different social roles in varied contexts (Burke, 1981).

Higgins (1987) developed a model that could predict emotional vulnerability stemming from contradictions between five categories of self beliefs: an actual or real self, an ideal self of personal values, an ought-to-be self that one felt a duty to be because of others, a can-do self with beliefs about skills, and a future self. The ideal self, sought as a personal goal, might not be the same as the ought-to-be self, sought for the self by others. Both might be different from a realistic expectation of self. In empirical studies, Higgins found that a large discrepancy between an actual and ideal self was related to symptoms of depression. An actual and ought-to-be discrepancy was related to symptoms of anxiety (Avants, Margolin, & Singer, 1993; Strauman & Higgins, 1987). These findings supported Freud's (1923) earlier theories about the negative emotional consequences of a mismatch between beliefs for an ego ideal and realistic appraisals of self. Depression occurred if the mismatch indicated a hopeless discord, anxiety if a future lapse was anticipated, and guilt or shame if criticism was in the air.

It is now generally agreed that the search for self-esteem is a powerful motivation. Lapses in a sense of self evoke, and are evoked by, negative emotions. For example, people with losses feel sad and sometimes self impaired. In a research study those who felt self-impaired had extended and turbulent grief reactions (Horowitz, Sonneborn, Sugahara, & Maercker, 1996; Horowitz, Milbrath, Bonnano et al, in press). In a different study, with another population, people with more conflictual or impoverished supraordinate schemas were less able to use exploratory psychotherapy to reduce the distress of their pathological grief reactions (Horowitz, Marmar, Weiss, DeWitt, & Rosenbaum, 1984). Similar findings were reported from other research groups by C. Anderson (1983), Kalthoff and Neimeyer (1993), and Piper, Azim, Joyce, & McCallum (1991b). Harmonious and well developed supraordinate self schemas help people react more resiliently to stress, and to cope better with traumatic events, coping well, and learning how to cope well, with traumatic events may also help people integrate divergent elements within self organization.

DEVELOPMENT

Early childhood experiences in relationships are important in establishing an initial set of self-concepts. The earliest precursors may even be prenatal. Identity experiences can become more complex through developments during every epoch of the life cycle. This view was held by Freud (1903), Abraham (1924), Klein (1948), Erikson (1950, 1958, 1959), Jacobson (1964), Mahler (1968), Bowlby (1969, 1973), and Kohut (1972, 1977). One of the most influential people to chart identity development over the life cycle was Erikson (1950, 1958, 1959). He provided a chart on the sequence of early childhood, and later on the adult development of identity. His final version is shown in Table 5.1, but it is in need of revision based on subsequent research on development (Damon, 1988; Emde, 1981, 1983; Franz & White, 1985; F. Horowitz, 1987; Singer, 1987; Stern, 1985). Table 5.2 is such a revision.

Erikson's chart emphasizes Freud's (1903) psychosexual theory or oral, anal, and genital derivatives of instinctual energy in the id. This theory is outmoded. The strength of Erikson's work, however, is his conceptualization of how individual traits might develop in different social contexts (and with different temperaments) over the entire life cycle. While Erikson investigated identity, he did not use person schemas theory of multiple selves. The strong form of conceptualization he advanced can be retained, with revision of the conceptual contents, that is why, in Table 5.2, I revised the epochs of the life cycle and focused on just identity developmental sequences. I will address Erikson's concern for relationships and character, using this same format in the next two chapters.

Erikson's work has been widely taught because the dichotomies he suggested—trust versus mistrust, autonomy versus shame and doubt, and initiative versus guilt—speak profoundly about the human predicament as presented in *Oedipus Rex* by Sophocles and *Hamlet* by Shakespeare. The basic strengths he covers—hope, will, purpose, competence, fidelity, love, care, and wisdom—are virtues people seek in establishing affectional ties to others, and traits they try to develop in themselves, over a lifetime. I followed Erikson's form of a polarity between adaptive and maladaptive traits in constructing Table 5.2. I focus first on beliefs of self versus fragmented ideas and then on competent and incompetent self schemas. The arc of growing self organization then encompasses, successively, multiple self schemas, configurations, supraordinate schemas, and overall self-organization.

INFANCY

Hope in a future for the self develops in the normal infant who receives adequate care. Research has shown that the better and more consistent the care, the greater the possibility for developing a sense of security (Ainsworth, 1973; Bowlby, 1969; Main, 1975). First beliefs about self develop in this matrix of good care from others (Stern, 1985). These first beliefs about self as a surviving entity are implicit rather than explicit, and probably evolve from innate precursors as a procedural kind of knowledge.

TABLE 5.1
ERIKSON'S CHART OF DEVELOPMENT

Stages	A. Psychosexual Stages and Modes	B. Psychosexual Crises	C. Radius of Significant Relationships	D. Basic Strengths	E. Core Pathology Basic Antipathies	F. Related Principles of Social Order	G. Binding Rationalizations	H. Ritualism
I. Infancy	Oral-respiratory, sensory-kinesthetic (incorporative modes)	Basic trust versus basic mistrust	Maternal person	Hope	Withdrawal	Cosmic order	Numinous	Idolism
II. Early Childhood	Anal-urethral, muscular (retentive-eliminative)	Autonomy versus shame, doubt	Parental persons	Will	Compulsion	"Law and order"	Judicious	Legalism
III. Play Age	Infantile-genital, locomotor (intrusive, inclusive)	Initiative versus guilt	Basic family	Purpose	Inhibition	Ideal prototypes	Dramatic	Moralism
IV. School Age	"Latency"	Industry versus inferiority	"Neighborhood," school	Competence	Inertia	Technological order	Formal (technical)	Formalism

108

	A	B	C	D	E	F	G	H
Stages	Psychosexual Stages and Modes	Psychosexual Crises	Radius of Significant Relationships	Basic Strengths	Core Pathology Basic Antipathies	Related Principles of Social Order	Binding Rationalizations	Ritualism
V. Adolescence	Puberty	Identity versus inferiority	Peer groups and outgroups, models of leadership	Fidelity	Repudiation	Ideological worldview	Ideological	Totalism
VI. Young Adulthood	Genitality	Intimacy versus isolation	Partners in friendship, sex, competition, cooperation	Love	Exclusivity	Patterns of cooperation and competition.	Affiliative	Elitism
VII. Adulthood	(Procreativity)	Generativity versus stagnation	Divided labor and shared household	Care	Rejectivity	Currents of education and tradition	Generational	Authoritism
VIII. Old Age	(Generalization of sensual modes)	Integrity versus despair	"Mankind" "My kind"	Wisdom	Disdain	Wisdom	Philosophical	Dogmatism

Source: Erikson 1982, pp. 32–33.

TABLE 5.2
LIFE THEMES AND IDENTITY FORMATION

Period of Life	Personal Tasks and Social Expectations	Identity
1. Infancy	Achieve attunement and secure attachments to other people; elicit affection; learn to walk and talk; acquire self-regulation	First beliefs about self (versus fragmented ideas)
2. Early Childhood	Increase bodily control; develop sense of right and wrong; learn communication skills; learn to negotiate; develop capacity for play and imagination; connect gender beliefs	Sense of competence of self; gender identification; beliefs about various possible selves (versus incompetence)
3. Middle Childhood	Experiment with sensuality; relate to peers; form close friendships; learn to work on one's own; enlarge sense of morality	Multiple self schemas and flexible confident shifts between them (versus rigidity and self-doubt)
4. Early Adolescence	Accept one's changing body; experiment with love and sexuality; forge peer groups; develop work and recreational abilities; differentiate ideal and real social practices	Develop more self schemas and use them resiliently (versus identity diffusion)
5. Late Adolescence	Improve modulation of emotion; extend understanding of gender and sexual roles; develop specific skills; learn to balance cooperation and independence	Supraordinate self schemas (versus dissociations)
6. Young Adulthood	Relate self to social systems of work and new families or groups	Harmonious configurations of self schemas (versus continued dissociations or conflictual configurations)
7. Middle Adulthood	Accept bodily declines; give to older and younger generation; transmit skills	Self-organization and hierarchy of personal values (versus self-disgust)
8. Late Adulthood	Accept aged body; adapt to retirement; confront transience; pass on leadership; transmit values	Wisely reschematized self-organization (versus terror or rage at ending life)

EARLY CHILDHOOD

As sensation, motor control, and movement experiences of the body and surrounding objects are coordinated, associational connections are established. Certain linkage patterns establish the first self schemas. As thought develops further, these working models of the body are connected with ideas and feelings that can be represented. The individual learns what the self can do and feel and differentiates that from what others do and feel. The infant, however, is so attuned to caregivers that it requires a reflectance from the other as to what the infant feels and does. A caregiver shows the baby not only what the caregiver feels but also what the baby feels. Apt, empathic, realistic, growth-promoting reflectance of emotions establish self-concepts in the child.

Children experiment constantly; play is their work. It is as if they are fueled by a burning question: What can I make happen? The child remembers what works, and how it works. Over time, a generalized model of "I" and "what I can do" is formed. Hope for a future self, then, has a basic root in first experiences that teach the individual when to count on the self and when to count on others.

MIDDLE CHILDHOOD

From the coherence and aptness of these first beliefs, established in infancy, a happy child displays signs of an ebullient self-confidence, reflecting competent schemas. Socially, others restrain the child from dangerous, inappropriate, or embarrassing actions and the child learns concepts of alternative self-actions. A variety of experiences then lead to the assembly of a repertoire of multiple self schemas by middle childhood. If repeated or traumatic social and environmental experiences convince a child that he or she is incompetent, damaged self schemas can result. As multiple self schemas develop, some may be used defensively to avoid dreaded states.

As a result of the linkage of beliefs about self with other mental knowledge, the child forms more global self schemas during middle childhood, as shown in Table 5.2. Conscious reflection on self can occur. Flexible shifts between schemas allow the child to sometimes be dependent on parents and, at other times, less dependent. This may be associated with reflective conscious experiences and judgments about what can be undertaken with competence and what should not be undertaken because of dependency. The balance between the self's realistic and unrealistic appraisals to perform various feats competently leads to self-confidence versus rigidity and self-doubt in middle childhood.

EARLY ADOLESCENCE

Vital change in gender characteristics occur as sexual hormones surge. A great deal of looking and awareness of being seen fuels new self conceptualizations and body images. Other people shift in importance. Nonetheless, the development of self-reflective abilities means that the person is not so dependent on being tied to or periodically reunited with parental figures, provided that self confidence can be sustained with less frequent parental attunement, monitoring, control, or reflectance (Emde, 1988; F. Horowitz, 1987). The adolescent gains resilience in roles. Relatively safe risks are taken in order to learn more about new potential roles. Peer groups become important as aids and lessen need for parental feedback. The person may, however, become excessively dependent on the peer group. A few persons may numbly conform to the will of leaders or the ritual practices of a group; others may take dangerous risks. Identity diffusion experiences might otherwise occur.

LATE ADOLESCENCE

In late adolescence, further associational linkages between self schemas develop, leading to integrative configurations. The person can safely have multiple self-concepts because supraordinate schemas provide coherence. The alternative to a rich multiplicity in self-appraisal may be dissociative experiences, of having not only different identity experiences but different styles, values, and memories in different states. Explosive state shifts may surprise and frighten companions. Or a veneer of normal traits may cloak a secret chaos at the heart of identity.

Although some adolescents use safe risk taking to explore possible new roles for self and possible routes through the maze of the world, a few adolescents, who cannot envision any safe or satisfying path use dangerous risk taking. A more desperate search for identity occurs. Erikson's (1958), study of clinical cases of such adolescents suggested that even a negative or antisocial identity was better than a sense of diffusion or chaos.

One reason for this choice was given in the myth of Lucifer, who preferred to reign in hell rather than serve in heaven: Destruction can be easier, quicker, and more startling to others than patient, creative, and constructive effort. Biologically, some adolescents may have a lower-than-normal capacity for schematizing complex self schemas. Psychologically, some adolescents may have trouble building such schemas on a base of damaged early self-concepts or troubled environments.

Socially, some adolescents may be placed in situations where available roles do not offer acceptable routes to a sense of a competent self. When social conditions are harsh to adolescents, it is more likely that late adolescents will choose dramatic, risky, and possibly destructive roles. In addition, the use of late adolescents as military men prematurely exposes them to warrior identities that then do not well suit some of them when they return to civilian life.

YOUNG ADULTHOOD

By young adulthood, a person can have integrated and supraordinate self schemas. These foster conscious experiences of identity, accepting contradictory self-concepts without excessive alarm reactions or consternation. The individual does not have to use extreme, reality-distorting defenses to alter negative self-appraisals. On the other hand, people with highly conflictual configurations are susceptible to states of self-disgust.

MIDDLE ADULTHOOD

By middle adulthood, even more integrative self-organizations can form. Complex networks of personal meaning establish a hierarchy of stable and personal values. This hierarchy of values makes decision making easier, even in stressful moral contexts the person knows what is good, and what is better. Enduring self-critical schemas can appraise self as worthy and lead to states of pride and pleasure in having been a good and effective person.

The physical body changes with injuries and aging. The changing expressions of genes and the physiology of the brain alters cognition, emotion, and reactivity to stress. Chemical alterations change sensitivities to others and urges towards others (Cloninger, 1990; Derryberry & Rothbart, 1988; Goldsmith & Campos, 1982). Social changes

shift the importance of individual roles. People with flexible and harmonious configurations modify self schematizations to keep up with
such changes. Persons with rigid identities cannot keep up as well.
Gaps between desired and real self-concepts widen and lead to self
disgust.

LATE ADULTHOOD

As late adulthood approaches, rich identity experiences protect the
person from being shattered by failures, losses, and declines. Personal transience can be accepted and a courageous face turned toward the inevitable demise of the consciously experiencing self. Only
some people ever achieve this stance, which can reduce terror and
rage with the realization of increasing physical disability and even an
increased chance of dying.

ANTICIPATING THE FUTURE

Children imagine future selves when they play. From early adolescence on, people can usefully experiment with a variety of possible
future selves in reflective consciousness (Blos, 1979; Fairbairn, 1954;
Guntrip, 1961; Higgins, 1987; Sarnoff, 1976; Winnicott, 1958). In an
imagined future of the self, some roles, scripts, body images, and values are kept, and others are reschematized or rejected. Dreaded and
desired futures are fantasized. The ideal and the real are compared
and contrasted. Schemas of these various possible futures evolve.
These cognitive maps and plans have motivational impact; people
avoid some and approach others. These schemas are used by preconscious processors that compute how present circumstances can lead
to possible futures.

Anticipating the future well can lead to flexibility rather than
rigidity. Beliefs about self are dynamic rather than static because life
itself is viewed as dynamic rather than static. Identity requires many
revisions for adaptive functioning over the entire life cycle, the work
is completed only with death.

SUMMARY

People want to experience coherence and clarity about who they are
and what their lives mean. They want to be understood and re-

spected by others as unique individuals. They want to attain good identity experiences despite realistic recognition of their own human inconsistencies and contradictions. However, to avoid dreaded or incoherent identity experiences, they may defensively activate compromise self schemas. Such defensive stances when habitually used can interfere with the development of self-organization. The character traits rigidity, timidity, dissociation, and neurotic immaturity may result.

Contradictory traits occur in people all the time. But connections can be made between even polar-opposite beliefs. Competing intentions and expectations can be linked together. Self-organization can become richer and more complex, more integrated, and more differentiated through the formation of supraordinate schematization. However, enrichment of identity usually occurs in the context of meaningful relationships.

CHAPTER 6

Relationships

THE COMPANIONSHIP of others is desired, sought after, and needed: It ensures survival. People want the safety, cooperation, sex, warmth, love, competitive stimulation, and reflections of identity that relationships can provide. Yet many people operate in ways that form and then break affectional ties, causing boredom, despair, or fear of abandonment.

Some people have a pattern of repeatedly destroying relationships because of acts driven by envy, rivalry, betrayal, power lust, inattention, or derision, or by being demanding or excessively dependent. Most people, at some time in their lives, distort thoughts and feelings in the arena of love, they may act immaturely and behave in ways that damage both self and others. Some people involuntarily and compulsively repeat patterns they hated in their own parents. Others disrupt their careers by expressive cowering, selfishness in regard to money, status, and work, or by focusing excessively on revenge.

Many aspects of beliefs about relationships operate as unconscious person schemas. At times, everyone behaves irrationally in a relationship and does not know how or why this happens. In psychotherapy, one goal is to gain awareness and insight into the underlying maladaptive schemas, changing the patterns by training and offering new choices, and encouraging new practices.

The heart can yearn for a new opportunity, but the mind might still repeat a cycle that ends in distress. Knowing what to change requires formulations about how unconscious intentions and expectations infuse person schemas. The procedural knowledge, learned in childhood and adolescence by associations formed without reflective consciousness now can be examined by transforming the patterns observed into declarative knowledge. Such formulations can bring clarity into an otherwise murky emotional domain.

Schools of psychotherapy offer theories about how to arrive at such formulations (Eells, 1997; Horowitz, 1997). Different schools have different theories. An integration across schools has become possible because of the emergent general agreement on the high importance of intrapsychic models that include roles for self and other. These intrapsychic codings of the social world have both roles for self and other and transactional scripts for interaction (Allport, 1955; Jacobson, 1964; Lewin, 1935; Murray, 1938). The patterned assembly of these intrapsychic elements in person schemas can be formulated as a role relationship model (Horowitz, 1979b, 1989a, b, 1991a, 1997b).

THE ROLE-RELATIONSHIP MODEL

A role relationship model (RRM) is a format used to define a recurrent pattern in a narrative or observed transaction (Berne, 1961; Carlson, 1981; Colby, Jessor, & Shweder, 1996; Horowitz, 1979b, 1989a, 1991a; Minsky, 1980; Tomkins, 1962). The elements include traits of self and others; transactional scripts for emotions, acts, and communications; and values used for critical appraisals of the consequences of a transaction. This RRM format is illustrated in Figure 6.1. An RRM is an assembly of associated meanings. This network of beliefs is a whole pattern larger than the sum of its parts. A format for assembling the pattern of self schema and a schema for another into a two-person RRM is illustrated in Figure 6.1. Figures could be made more complex for multi-person depictions; one could make a map for three, four, or more people. This RRM format evolved empirically. Judges of recorded clinical research data could arrive at an agreement of inferences, while independently reviewing the same case material (Eells, et al., 1995; Horowitz & Eells, 1993; Horowitz, Eells, Singer, & Salovey, 1995). Similar results have been found in research using an alternative format called a *core conflictual relationship theme* (Luborsky & Crits-Christoph, 1990); and accord has been found with yet other analagous systems (Horowitz, 1991).

Internalized maps, blueprints, or person schemas include *working models* of a current situation and *enduring schemas* generalized from

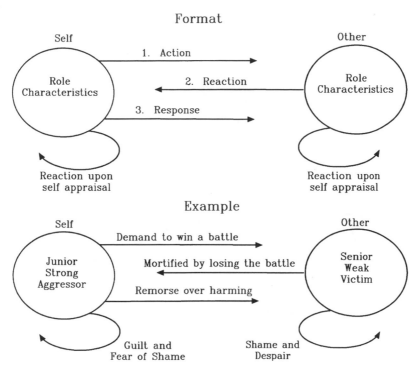

FIGURE 6.1

A Format for an RRM and One Example

past relationships. As previously discussed, a working model* is an interpretation of the present. A working role-relationship model is formed from dual sources: observation of what is happening now in an interpersonal situation and information from a RRM activated from a repertoire of enduring self-other schemas.

Various processes combine to form working models, as illustrated in Figure 6.2. The bold arrow in Figure 6.2 indicates that one role-relationship model is likely to be primed as a main source for organizing a working model in a current state.

In Figure 6.2, the social transaction contributes to, and is influenced by, the working model. Only one working model is shown to

---

*I use the term *working model* to mean the currently active schematic organization of beliefs. This is analogous to the construct of working memory in cognitive science. Bowlby (1973) has been very important in the development of person schemas theory, but I should note that he used this term somewhat differently. He contrasted *working* with *nonworking* models. Nonworking models, once formed, were not changed by current cognitive processes. Working models could be changed by new information (Aubrey Metcalf, M.D., personal communication, August, 1997).

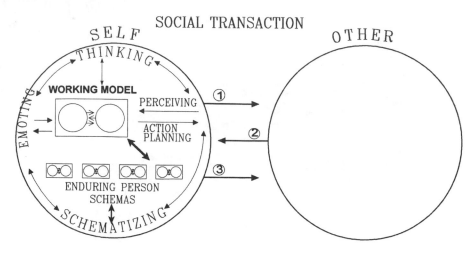

FIGURE 6.2
WORKING MODEL OF A SOCIAL TRANSACTION

avoid complexity; however, multiple working models are probably active in parallel processors. Some might conform well to the actual ongoing situation and its opportunities, and others might deviate from such realities. Some working models might be quite irrational and contribute seemingly aberrant elements to the unfolding social relationship.

An attachment to a significant other might be experienced differently at different times and in different states of mind. Sometimes these differences are due to activation of separate enduring person schemas. Figure 6.2 shows several enduring and alternatively available RRMs. Each could be used in forming a working model, and each could lead to certain emotional, wishful, and fearful colorations of a state of mind. Ambivalent attachments, for example, might have a configuration of RRMs, some prone to evoke hate, others love or feigned indifference. All might be part of a configuration of person schemas.

Perceptions and emerging intentions/expectations about a relationship can be processed in parallel. Different schemas provide different templates. Each template connects bits of information by different associational patterns that, when processed in parallel, lead to alternative appraisals of possible relationship futures. Several enduring person schemas might be activated, each organizing different parallel processors. However, conscious reflection tends to be dominated by only one of the person schemas. When several person schemas influence mood and emotion, the results may be shimmering states.

Unconscious interpretations, intentions, and expectations of a relationship are, in part, based on person schemas. In psychotherapy, beliefs contained inchoately may be raised to awareness and insight. This process of awareness and insight usually requires self-observation as well as self-experience, in a state of reflective consciousness.

The observing self in a state of reflective consciousness can become aware of having more than one working model. This occurs through conscious representations of derivatives of each of several models. A person could check his or her actual situation to see if one working model had an irrational or inappropriate belief and another had a rational or more salient belief. Insight about the differences between the sets of beliefs could clarify a new social opportunity. The person could decide to steer into new waters.

A new social transaction could be tried. Making new decisions and repeating new behaviors could lead to processes of reschematization. The outcome of these processes would be a revised person schema and, perhaps, a better developmental integration of existing configurations of role-relationship models (Horowitz, 1991, 1992; Horowitz, Marmar, Krupnick, et al., 1984; Stern, 1985).

CONFIGURATIONS OF ROLE-RELATIONSHIP MODELS

Supraordinate schemas can contain several role relationship models, and the combination is called a *configuration*. The shift from one RRM to another leads to a shift in state, and repetitions of a sequence of shifts produces a cycle of states. An example is a person in a state of *brimming with love*, who, fearing rejection, shifts to a *timid and tense* state. The *timid and tense* state shimmers with signs of interest but also expressions that stifle love. A dreaded state of *shame* on rejection is warded off, but so is the opportunity for affection. The person may then shift from the *timid and tense* state to a *sullen and apathetic* state. This can be followed by a search for renewed closeness, beginning the cycle again in a *brimming with love* state. This cycle, with its episodes of withdrawal and sullenness, does not provide satisfaction for either party. The complexity of such cycles makes insight difficult to achieve. We can clarify the pattern, however, by unpacking the several role relationship models that operate as a configuration, as in the following example.

André

André, as an adolescent, had fantasies about the roles that he might take in his anticipated future relationships with women. One of André's states of mind was *romantic spirituality*. His role-relationship model for this state had a self schema of a good and heroic young man. The script in this model engaged him in mutual admiration with a lovely young woman. These roles contradicted those in André's state of *erotic lust*. In this state, his fantasies cast him as a strong, brutal man taking advantage of a weaker but enthralled woman. In another fantasy, he reversed roles: In a state of *passive eroticism*, he cast himself as an inexperienced, captured, attractive boy being sexually exploited by a powerful woman who cast a spell over him, tied him up, and caressed his body.

As an adult, André combined these role-relationship models into a script-like sequence. The repetition of this cycle became apparent during the stories he told during psychotherapy. In the beginning of a cycle, he would approach an attractive woman and organize his emotions and fantasies by the romantic model. In this stance, he would save her from other men who might only want her as a sex object. He expected her to love him for his purity. During intercourse, however, he felt that he was defiling her. After sexual intercourse, his appraisals again changed. He viewed her as domineering and demanding; he feared she would control and smother him, and he began to hate her. These feelings caused him to end the relationship. The script involved approaching, saving, defiling, hating, and then ending the relationship; it became a repeated cycle.

André tended to stereotype women as either good or bad. With good women he was less able to feel erotic because he believed they regarded sex as dirty; with them he felt guilt or shame. With bad women he was unable to feel warm and close because he believed they were worthless and out to trap him, to regard him as their possession. André fought a wish–fear dilemma about women in each new romantic engagement. The dilemma had a configuration of various RRMs that led to various defensive compromises.

SYSTEMATIC FORMULATION

Desired, dreaded, and defensive role-relationship models for a given theme form a configuration. A systematic format that has been found useful for formulating an RRM configuration is illustrated in Figure

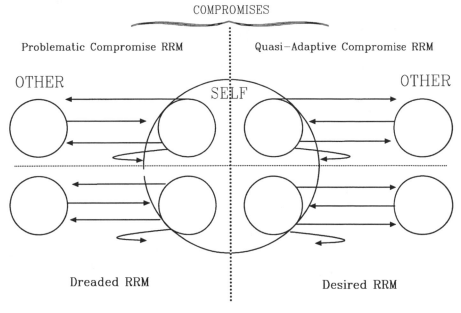

WISH-FEAR DILEMMA

FIGURE 6.3
A Configuration of RRMs

6.3; it uses the familiar quadratic layout. The configuration of RRMs is organized with self schemas in a central circle of self-organization.

The entire lower half of the configuration contains a wish–fear dilemma—the emotionally charged *desired* and *dreaded* role-relationship models. The dreaded role-relationship model in the lower-left quadrant of the configuration relates to feared consequences of the desired acts. RRMs in the upper half of the configuration organize defensive states that ward off the wish–fear dilemma of the bottom half. If the compromise RRM organizes states of mind with problematic emotions or symptoms, it is called a *problematic compromise*. If these emotions, ideas, and actions of a state are attenuated but the person still must avoid full satisfactions, it is called a *quasi-adaptive compromise*. In this case, *quasi* refers to the inference that a better adaptation could conceivably be reached in the future. Such configurations of RRM are illustrated in the case of Carl.

Carl

Carl was in early middle age and suffered from states of depression, loneliness, and self-disgust. He was unable to form long-term relationships, feeling that others walled him off. After awhile, it became clear that although loneliness caused him suffering, Carl was even more frightened of being abandoned. If he were left by someone, he would enter a state of profound despair, which was much worse than loneliness.

Carl's childhood experiences were pertinent. At about the age of 4, Carl was abandoned by his mother for 6 months. When he was 12 years old, his father died. At the time he did not mourn; he stood aloof from his mother at his father's funeral. Chastised by her for his lack of concern, he ignored her and felt self-sufficient.

Carl did well in school and, because of athletic prowess, was given a college scholarship. He completed his bachelor's degree and post-graduate education. After finding lucrative employment, his career advanced smoothly.

Carl had *exhilarated* states of mind, especially if he was showing off, but his pleasure in this was unstable. A mere glance from another person or a shift of attention away from him would stifle his exhilaration. He was never deeply committed to friends and his sexual liaisons were brief.

Carl sought psychotherapy in the second decade of his work life. During his treatment, he mourned his father, which was a surprising development so many years after his death. During an early phase of this work, as a transference reaction, Carl threatened to leave therapy and imagined that his therapist would be sad. Carl came to believe that the therapist could tolerate losing Carl despite missing him. In a second phase of this work, when the therapist went away on vacation, in another transference reaction, Carl missed him and felt intensely sad. He realized that he was the one concerned with separations. After that, vivid memories from the time of his father's death occurred and, for a time, Carl felt distressed that he had lost his father before they had ever connected as adults.

As he became convinced that the therapist would stay in a consistent relationship with him, his fears of becoming close to another person were revealed. He became able to recognize and discuss his fear of experiencing an undermodulated and *horrific despair* if he were abandoned. He then learned to counteract his automatic tendency to withdraw from closeness. He began to risk deeper relationships with peers; he eventually developed friendships, and then a close sexual relationship.

Carl explored a triangle of personal meaning involving himself, his mother, and his father. In some states, he viewed the relationship between his mother and father, or current figures that might fit into these schemas, as ones between heroes and heroines. In that scenario, his mother was an ideal woman married to a loving tough guy like Humphrey Bogart. This idealized model of his parents stood in stark contrast to the unconscious model developed out of his traumatic experiences. That model included his mother as a shattered and absent caretaker and his father as a vulnerable man who died suddenly. If Carl was like his father, he too could suffer a sudden death. If he was to rely on his mother, she might abandon him at any moment. The trauma of abandonment led to despair that he might lose a person essential to his safety and development. He came through adolescence in a state of defensiveness against this despair. By being a self-sufficient loner, he thought he would protect himself. Some of Carl's contradictory beliefs and conflicted identifications are illustrated in Figure 6.4.

Carl often used a quasi-adaptive *aloof* state as a character trait. This prevented romances from deepening to intimacy. He regarded himself as a self-sufficient man and viewed attractive and eligible women as unreliable companions. This attitude prevented worry

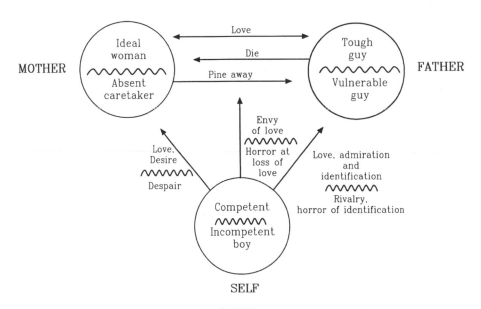

FIGURE 6.4

Carl's Triangular and Conflictual RRM

Important contradictions are indicated with a wavy line.

about rejection or abandonment. This quasi-adaptive compromise RRM is shown in the upper-right quadrant of Figure 6.5. Carl recognized this character trait and began to see it as alien to his wishes for mutual love and admiration in an ideal relationship. The desired RRM is shown in the lower-right quadrant of Figure 6.5.

Grief work in therapy helped Carl mourn his father; he then felt less frightened of intimacy. He was ready for a suitable companion. He became acquainted with a woman and then fell deeply in love. Mutual excitement occurred; each one idealized the other. The affair quickly reached a high level of intensity. He and his beloved formed a *love nest*: They spent every possible minute together and wanted no contact with anyone else. Carl experienced a delightful sense of calm, as well as periods of high sexual excitement, in this relationship.

Carl's desired state of love and pride, however, was still linked to a dreaded state in which he felt *despair* that he would be abandoned. When his lover wanted contact with her relatives and previous best friend, Carl felt so neglected that he entered into a state of *despair*. His self schema was of a totally vulnerable boy, one ripped open and

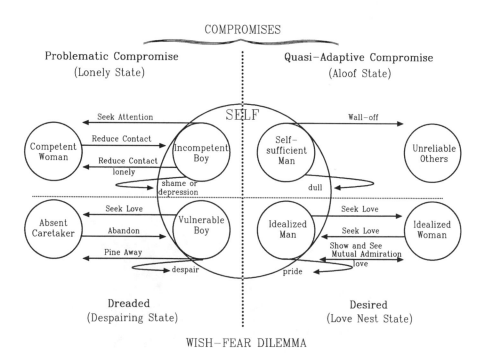

WISH–FEAR DILEMMA

FIGURE 6.5

CARL'S RRM CONFIGURATION FOR THE THEME OF INTIMACY

beaten down by the abandonment of an essential but absent care-taker. This is depicted in the RRM in the lower-left quadrant of Figure 6.5. To ward off his distress, Carl shifted into a problematic compromise *lonely* state, shown in the upper-left quadrant of Figure 6.5.

In his *lonely* state, fears of *despair* were less intense. He viewed himself as incompetent at keeping the attention of a loved one. He saw his lover as a competent woman who found him less competent than herself, a distortion of her actual motives. He felt irrationally ashamed that he could not keep her interest at an exalted level. He felt depressed as well as lonely. To reduce the distressing emotions of his *lonely* state, he shifted his self schema to that of a competent, self-sufficient man. He regarded his woman friend as unreliable; he walled her off. Once again, he entered a defensively *aloof* state and regressed to his character trait of the self-sufficient man.

Carl had a somewhat similar cycle at his place of work. The related configuration of RRMs is shown in Figure 6.6. In his desired state, he wanted to cooperate with coworkers whom he idealized. Connection

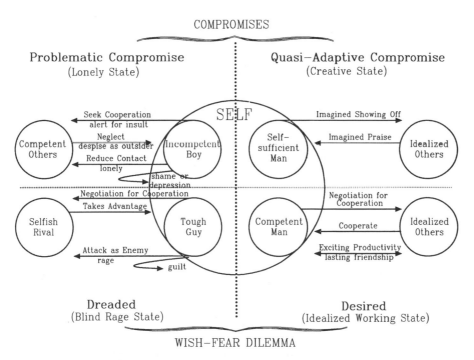

FIGURE 6.6

CARL'S RRM CONFIGURATION FOR THE THEME OF WORK

with these fine people would replace what he had lost when his idealized father died. But negotiating closely risked priming of a dreaded role-relationship model. He had a wish–fear dilemma: If he showed coworkers his plans, they might cooperate closely with him, but they might also steal them, take advantage of him, and become enemies rather than allies.

Carl felt distrust of others. He tested them with provocations to see if, as he expected, they would take advantage of him. Whenever he felt as though others were attacking and seeking to injure him because of his vulnerabilities, he flew into an uncontrolled *blind rage*. He frequently felt misused and provoked others in ways that really did lead to their attacking him. After a *blind rage* state erupted, he felt self-disgust, shame, rejection, and guilt for his excessive retaliations. These negative emotions led him to shift into the problematic compromise state of *loneliness*, which was organized by an incompetent self schema and a script of avoidance of expected rejection.

The dreaded state contained a self schema as a tough guy, derived from his identification with his father. Carl's father was too tough, a bit crazy in his own rages, irrationally inflating competitive situations into ones in which one party might be annihilated. Carl was afraid of lapsing into a similar self schema, which he viewed as terribly dangerous. To avoid this situation, he shifted his state of mind from *blind rage* to *loneliness*. This was accomplished by control processes that shifted his self schema from tough guy to incompetent boy. That change reduced his rage by counteracting hostility with fear of hostility.

In his problematic compromise role-relationship model, he expected others would neglect him rather than cooperate with him; after all, they were competent and he was incompetent. To avoid this expected rejection, he reduced contact with them, shifting to his quasi-adaptive compromise state. He could then change to a self-sufficient and manly self schema and imagine himself making great work products and showing them off, with a fantasy of praise that sustained his positive affect. When alone, this view could promote a *creative* state.

He could then attempt his desired state of *idealized working* with others, but it was seldom reached in real transactions. When this desired state did not happen, he shifted to the problematic compromise state and sought cooperation, but in a weak way that avoided the tough-guy self schema that might lead to his rage. In the weak role of incompetent boy, he was ever on the alert for insults, making him an overly defensive and thus undesirable companion.

People like Carl have role-relationship models that were developed in childhood that influence their adult states of mind. In psychotherapy, and by his diligent efforts to increase his awareness of real possibilities for affiliating with others, Carl was able to reschematize his identity and his repertoire of person schemas.

DEVELOPMENT

The development of relationship schemas is probably one of the most complex mental activities. While considerable research on this topic has been reported, the relevant pathways are still in part mysterious (Emde, 1981, 1983; Greenspan & Lourie, 1981; F. Horowitz, 1987; Stern, 1985). The layout of Table 6.1 summarizes a possible sequence from birth to late life. The same periods of life and the same personal tasks and social expectations as used for self development (Chapter 5, Table 5.2) provide the sequence. The kind of lifelong development depicted is possible, but not certain. Each person can mature and flower, or fixate and stagnate. Damaged people can form strange paths and variously distorted relationship schemas. But the essential fact is that people, even in the midst of stagnation, and even later in life, can change by learning how to reschematize their repertoire of beliefs.

INFANCY

The emergence of consciousness and the formation of self schemas occur in the safety and love provided by caregivers. This first understanding of relationships is provided by memories of expressions, bodily touch, and vocal sounds as basic needs are met or neglected. Caregivers who are inconsistent, who use the baby as a tool for their own purposes without regard to its humanity and incipient soul, fail the infant. The result is development of impoverished relationship schemas of the most primal sort. But damaged or impoverished relationship schemas are also influenced by the baby: Infants with abnormal brain function may be underschematized or undercontrolled in self-organization.

Later schematizations of relationship patterns can sometimes compensate for such early damage. Nonetheless, the person who sur-

TABLE 6.1
LIFE THEMES AND DEVELOPMENT OF RELATIONSHIP SCHEMAS

Period of Life	Personal Tasks and Social Expectations	Relationship Schemas
1. Infancy	Achieve attunement and secure attachments to other people; elicit affection and responses; learn to walk and talk; acquire self-regulation	First understanding of self with other (versus lack of self-regulation because of lack of regulation by other)
2. Early Childhood	Increase bodily control; develop sense of right and wrong; learn communication skills; learn to negotiate; developing capacity for play and imagination; connect gender beliefs	Roles for emotional interactions (versus deficits and conflicts)
3. Middle Childhood	Experiment with sensuality; relate to peers; form close friendships; learn to work on one's own; enlarge sense of morality	Multiple role relationship models of friendship, and rank; practices for leading, following, and doing work (versus apathy or stigmatization)
4. Early Adolescence	Accept one's changing body; experiment with love and sexuality; forge peer groups; develop work and recreational abilities; differentiate ideal and real social practices	Resilient use of alternative roles and scripts for sexuality, fighting, and commitments (versus relationship confusion)

Period of Life	Personal Tasks and Social Expectations	Relationship Schemas
5. Late Adolescence	Improve modulation of emotion; extend understanding of gender and sexual roles; develop specific skills; learn to balance cooperation and independence	Supraordinate role-relationship models (versus dissociations)
6. Young Adulthood	Relate to social systems of work and new families or groups	Harmonious supraordinate configurations of role-relationship models (versus continued dissociations and conflicted configurations leading to maladaptive but repeated relationship cycles)
7. Middle Adulthood	Accept bodily declines; give to older and younger generation; transmit skills	Relationship "cogwheelings" (versus contradictory relationships with older and younger generations)
8. Late Adulthood	Accepting aged body; adapt to retirement; confront transience; pass on leadership; transmit values	Schemas of the future in which concepts of the self and of valued relationships survive personal death (versus bitterness)

vives such early conditions may be more vulnerable than others to regression into dreaded states. That is, the person under stress may shift into states with a chaotic sense of shattered connection to others and a loss of identity sense.

EARLY CHILDHOOD

As the toddler gains knowledge about how to move, he or she recognizes who is in control. This realization further differentiates self from others. Capacities for play and imagination grow, and relationship schemas for gender differences form. Emotional interactions occur with parents, and words such as no and stop become as important as lullabies and cooing. Optimal restraint teaches adaptive self-regulation. Abuse, loss, and major inconsistencies may distress and confuse the child.

Schemas for desired and dreaded role relationships form; the child generalizes cognitive maps about what acts please and displease, propitiate and inflame, relax or stimulate others. Skills include script sequences of how to cooperate, compete, or elicit attention.

New roles are acquired, and embedded with complementary roles for others. Some children, however, acquire only an impoverished knowledge of how to connect to others. They develop and receive little empathy. Abuse, loss, and major inconsistency may confuse. Conflicts and wish–fear dilemmas can become schematized. Motives for restitution of losses or revenge for abuses can become so intense that they operate later in life as unconscious fantasies (Arlow, 1969; Knapp, 1991).

MIDDLE CHILDHOOD

As the child interacts with his or her peers, he or she learns friendship roles. Issues of personal status with regard to others are engaged. Practices of how to imitate evolve into procedures about how to lead and/or follow.

Schemas for group membership evolve in school, on the street, as well as in the family. Those who develop impoverished and conflicted role-relationship models tend to become apathetic and withdrawn. Whereas continued capability forges a "we schema" of self in a group, continued ineptitude leads to social ostracization and, perhaps, even to schemas of self as stigmatized. Roles of victimization and degradation may etch dreaded role-relationship models. Dreaded role-relationship models may require extreme compromises to avoid distressing affective states. Greater irrationality is both tolerated and needed as a defense to avoid yet greater dangers. Conflicted configurations form and then dispose the person to interpersonal problems later in life.

Early Adolescence

The early adolescent practices alternative roles for others, as well as self, in fantasy, observation, and action. Body images and scripts for sexual courtship evolve beyond early childhood experiments. Peer engagements reinforce masculine, feminine, and status-based roles and styles. Urges are strong in adolescence, but values are also firmed and generalized. Shall and shall-not rules are emphasized and critic roles evolve.

Flexibility in shifting roles and changing social situations is associated with harmonious configurations of RRMs. Deficits in person schemas can lead to identity diffusion and relationship confusion (Erikson, 1982; Jacobson, 1964). Adolescents who develop an impoverished repertoire, with damaged, deficient or rigid RRMs, may cement themselves into a deviant peer group in order to avoid the failure of not having enriching relationships (Sarnoff, 1976). Other socially limited adolescents may preconsciously evolve creative and imaginative skills as substitutes for actual companionship. They do well alone, but crumble with intimacy. Such problems may be transient, as a kind of "catch-up" development.

Late Adolescence

The late adolescent extends the social horizon to wider recognitions and forms more and more supraordinate schemas for relationships. Roles are established for apt transactions with people who are older, younger, more and less powerful or knowledgeable. The multiplicity of RRMs and the evolution of associational connections between alternative RRMs allows the adolescent to tolerate the mixtures of love and hate that can occur in a relationship. Alternatively, a person with intense negative RRMs and few alternative and supraordinate RRMs tends to enter explosive undermodulated emotional states when frustrated or threatened. These states often fracture a relationship, so the person must have multiple brief encounters to avoid isolation. These sudden shifts in state, due to impoverished supraordinate schemas, can also lead to dissociative behaviors, especially if the person has experienced many or very intense traumatic life events, losses, and abuses (Spiegel, 1994).

Young Adulthood

The young adult continues to learn wider roles by engaging in the world beyond school. New connections between varied roles continue to form and reschematize supraordinate configurations. The further development of RRM configurations leads to a repertoire of recurrent traits and states of mind. Other people recognize personality more clearly because of the repeated patterns in interpersonal behavior that are observed over time. Supraordinate configurations that are harmonious increase trust and commitment despite the limitations that occur in any enduring relationship.

The young adult can evolve an ever-expanding system of relationship beliefs. These can form well-integrated supraordinate schemas, leading to a more continuous sense of identity. Some can say, "I've got it together!" But most young adults feel, in this regard, that they have not yet done so. An understanding of person schemas can give them hope and a goal: Harmonious configurations can be learned through experience.

Integrated, harmonious RRM configurations allow for flexible changes in roles. This leads to poise and subtle nuances in any relationship. The person is able to take on diverse and fluctuating roles such as having a higher or lower status than others without a loss of commitment, responsibility, or personal freedom. If not, the person may continue dissociative behaviors and exhibit maladaptive relationship patterns.

Middle Adulthood

People hope to achieve the zenith of their social powers and affiliations during middle adulthood. Increase in status within a family and social group gives the person a wider scope for teaching younger people how to take on personal skills and responsibilities. Earlier losses, injuries, slights, and abuses can now be just another part of the individual stories that replicate the human condition. The compensations of successes, skills, attachments, wisdom, humor, and faith appease previously troubled hearts. Person schemas integrate key recurrent memories of the past with present goals and values for the future. More of the population, at this age, will be able to say "I've got it together."

In young adulthood, personal skill, work, prestige, power, fame, and money may be important goals. In middle adulthood, some people begin to view relationships as the most important aspect of their life. Many give friendship, love, and caretaking a priority over social status and the acquisition of wealth—if and when there is a conflict of intentions. Relationships that were conflicted in the past, or that have become deadened emotionally, are examined insightfully to see what can change.

Transferring roles and skills to the next generation can begin, and these acts increase or decrease self-esteem. The bodily declines that accompany age may lower self-regard; they can make a person feel too pressured by the loss of youth. Instead of cogwheeling well with older and younger people, a person may exhibit contradictory and age-inappropriate behavioral patterns, such as dressing like an adolescent. As a result, the person can become isolated from meaningful interactions with others.

LATE ADULTHOOD

Throughout life, schemas of time and of relationships over time, evolve. The person can have reflective consciousness about a life story involved with others. The horizon is sensed, death is anticipated, and a mastery of transience is not easy. The recognition of having limited time is unpleasant. A fear of dying occurs, as a dreaded state. In the mastery of this fear, concepts of relationships often deepen. The result of mastery may be conscious, reflective experiences based on projected future fantasies of how loved ones and valued institutions will survive the death of the self. Scripts of that survival are formed, leading to a conscious sense of continuity in the face of personal transience.

These experiences of the mastery of transience can reaffirm life.

Alternatively, contemplation of personal death can evoke bitterness. Erikson meant exactly this in his presentation of the crises of old age as polarity between integrity and despair.

RELATIONSHIP THEMES AND UNCONSCIOUS FANTASIES

Unconscious fantasies motivate many choices in life, especially the ones that are difficult to make. They produce recurrent themes and, sometimes, recurrent mistakes. These themes can braid through a life story without conscious recognition. Using reflective consciousness, people can understand their own themes, they can recall memories and link them in new ways. Without knowing why, people may recognize that they have been on a quest to save a parent, regain lost respect, right a wrong, acquire domination of those who once took their power, or restore an irretrievably lost love.

Unconscious and person schematic fantasies have been conceptualized in theoretical constructs called *templates* (Freud, 1912), *complexes* and *archetypes* (Charcot, 1877; Jung, 1959), *games* (Berne, 1961), *unconscious fantasies* (Arlow, 1969; Freud, 1915), *schemactive cores* (Knapp, 1991), *core conflictual relationship themes* (Luborsky, 1977), and *unconscious plans* (E. Weiss, 1960; J. Weiss & Sampson, 1986). These theories agree that early relationship beliefs can endure as motivations that effect current behavioral patterns without awareness.

People may schematize maladaptive unconscious fantasies when they seek as children to explain stressor events such as injuries, loss, abuse, or separations. For example, a child's parents may both love the child yet divorce for other reasons. One parent may obtain custody. The child may fantasize that the other parent has left because he or she does not love the child, or even that a bad act of self led to that imagined loss of love. The child may develop a cluster of dysfunctional beliefs such as "I have never been loved because I am, at the core, unlovable" (Beck, 1976; Wurmser, 1981).

The future is grim if the child believes "I shall never be loved," or "I am unlovable because I am weak, dirty, and defective and I will always be so." The theme may include beliefs about restitution or compensation. The child and then the adult may come to adapt a belief such as "I will only be acceptable if I discover a cure for cancer." The child, and then the adolescent, and then the adult, may plan heroic scientific research to convince others that the self is finally worthy of love.

A boy may want to be cuddled by his mother because he feels lonely; yet, at the same time, he may be ashamed that cuddling with mommy is only for babies, not for strong boys. To avoid ridicule, he may fantasize himself as a wounded soldier. This soldier role would entitle him to be nursed back to health by a caring woman. This RRM between nurse and wounded soldier is a compromise RRM. It is close enough to the initially desired RRM to satisfy his wish and far enough from the dreaded RRM that leads to ridicule. Later in life, the man may unconsciously seek to be injured as a means of being nursed.

Since future plans are often forged on the basis of childhood emotional investments, the unconscious goals may seem silly or illusory on adult awareness of the fantasy. This leads to a resistance to work that promotes insight into unconscious fantasies. Deeper understanding removes that resistance, with empathy for how the self felt as a child, and recognition of the continuing dynamics of early RRM configurations.

SUMMARY

Enduring person schemas influence the construction of a mental working model of each currently important relationship. These models organize how people interact and express feelings. Role-relationship models are an important type of person schema because they contain attributes of both self and others with script-like sequences for organizing intentions and expectations.

Role-relationship models are modified as an affectional tie deepens. New forms of experiences can lead to new role-relationship models. Supraordinate schemas develop, and these can integrate previously contradictory attitudes. These larger systems can soften prior tendencies to extremes of positive and negative behaviors in cyclic maladaptive relationship patterns. People can go from conflicted configurations of role-relationship models to a more harmonious balance. They can reduce the influence of previous unconscious fantasies and act on real opportunities for cooperation, friendship, and love.

CHAPTER 7

Character

MANY PEOPLE'S mental activities function like an internal scale that weighs their own needs with the needs of the people around them. One side of the scale holds a person's identity, and the other side holds his or her relationships with others. The balance is constantly shifting between these two sides, as people make selfish and selfless choices. When conflict arises, people consciously or unconsciously refer to their values in order to help them make decisions. A supraordinate framework with harmonized values indicates a mature and well-balanced character.

At birth, people already have the beginnings of their character in place; they have a biological predilection for a particular temperament. Their families are their first social environment and therefore play a role in their subsequent personality development. Later, in childhood and adolescence, outside influences also contribute to the formation of inner integrity. Then, as people develop during adulthood, they add more memories and experiences that help them to further define their character. They integrate previously disparate elements.

Understanding the character of another person is a component of trust. When people make alliances, they want to know how their partner will behave in a possible conflict: Will they sacrifice the alliance or preserve the partnership? This question is particularly important for people who are conferring power or choosing leaders. Voters want to know if candidates for public office will keep campaign promises or betray their constituencies for personal gain. Opponents target character weaknesses of rivals as evidence that the candidate will not be a force for the greater good. Intimations are made about private interests, deceits, and readily altered commitments.

Personality is often discussed along two dimensions: temperament and character (Cloninger, Svrakic, and Przyteck 1996). *Temperament* refers to prenatal "givens," such as genetic endowment and biological propensities. *Character* refers to what is learned; it is a psychosocial component. Character develops, and it is observed as a combination of identity and relationship patterns. Strength of character can be defined as a balancing integration of self-serving and group-serving goals.

Any relationship involves commitment to shared agreements, tacit or explicit. When a person establishes an alliance, he or she wants to know if the partner will stay affiliated, keep promises, or follow shared rules in a crisis. Character, to be good and solid in the socially accepted sense, requires more than self-service; it requires we-service.

In everyday life, people speak of character in a way that is not exactly the same as that of mental health professionals. Lay people give a high moral value to self-sacrifice: A mother who dies for her child, a friend who dies for another, and a bodyguard killed shielding his client are said to display good character. So, too, do martyrs who die for the faith and starving folk who do not steal bread. Character is moral—good or bad—and value judgments are made from the group's standpoint. In contrast, academic psychologists (Kohlberg, 1969; Loevinger, 1976) and mental health clinicians (Johnson, 1994; McWilliams, 1994) appraise values and commitments but do not center on social morality. Instead, they focus on inferred qualities of an inner integrity.

Integrity involves a balance between wants and shoulds, between impulses and self-regulations, and between the values of different relationships. These clinical appraisals are more complex and less judgmental than social estimates. The appraisals are made with the goal of helping the person develop his or her potential strength of character.

Clinicians use long-term psychotherapy or psychoanalysis to help people with character problems. Problems of character include meanness in the strong person, failure to produce in the creative person, fickleness in the attractive person, and self-abnegation in the easily led person. Several dimensions have been suggested that produce a bevy of typologies (Benjamin, 1991; Cloninger, 1990; Wiggens, 1982). Across these dimensions and typologies, issues of dominance versus submission, or autonomy versus excessive dependence, stand out as common themes.

Research in child development has suggested that some infants and children are more assertive and leading, and others are more readily fearful and shy. This difference in genetically determined temperaments (Cloninger, 1990; Kagan, 1982) may dispose some people toward insecurity during attachments, but parents' actions are equally or more important (Ainsworth, Blehar, Waters, & Wall, 1978; Bretherton & Waters, 1985; Emde, 1981, 1983; Main, 1975; Plomin & Dunn, 1986; Sroufe & Fleeson, 1986). The securely attached child tolerates separation from the mother. The anxiously attached child has less confidence and is more clinging. The combination of an anxiety-prone temperament and strain during early attachments could dispose a person to developing a clinging, dependent type of character problem (Blatt & Lerner, 1983; Bowlby, 1969, 1973; Bretherton, 1985; Erikson, 1950; Mayman, 1968; Spitz, 1960). Traits of timidity, lack of confidence, passivity, dependency, and clinging might manifest as a character structure during adolescence and young adulthood. But new experiences might also occur, and the person could learn different schemas of self-confidence and trust in relationships (Wolf, 1979).

A HISTORICAL PERSPECTIVE

Many eras have had their own approaches to reading character. The Greek philosopher Theophrastes (Eliot, 1994) wrote a book on the topic that is still read and referenced in modern philosophy classes. He defined and observed character in terms of specific traits. These traits were about identity and relationship maintenance over time.

Hippocrates focused on temperament in his treatise on four basic bodily humors. He linked psychological traits of moods to each biological temperament. He noted that inborn tendencies toward a hot temper, melancholy, phlegm, or passion might be modified by socialization. His was an early biopsychosocial model that focused on self and other transactional traits.

Aristotle (as translated in 1985) wrote about how facial features might indicate character: A face like a lion suggested powerful, imperious, cunning traits. Neomancers alleged that they could know character from the pattern of moles on the skin, phrenologists read character traits from bones of the skull, and cairomancers or palmists read character in the lines of the hand. Lavater wrote a book in 1776 incorporating such knowledge, and his alleged compendium on character influenced beliefs well into the nineteenth century (Krystal, 1994). Aristocrats were thought to have high brows, chins that were not too protuberant, lips that were thin, and noses that were fine. That physiognomy meant they could be expected to look ahead, do good, lead, and keep their word. The opposite might be the case of the peasantry, who were "born to their station," and supposedly had protuberant chins, thick lips, and stubby or broad noses. Thus, issues of dominance and subordination were emphasized in character readings.

Playwrights and novelists explored tragic flaws in character. Psychoanalysts explored how early development led to character themes that might persist throughout life (Brody, 1992; Kets de Vries & Perzow, 1991; McWilliams, 1994). In clinical psychoanalysis, technique grew to emphasize transference reactions as routes to unlock mysteries of character and unconscious fantasy. Impulsive tendencies and defenses against dreaded sexual and aggressive fantasies were clarified. The phenomena of transference and defensive control were seen as a reflection of a long-standing personality structure. Gradually, character modification became the prime target of psychoanalytic treatment (Baudry, 1984; Reich, 1949), and early character formation a topic of child observational studies (Brody, 1992; Greenspan, 1994).

Patterns of character pathology were, at first, classified in psychoanalytic studies as either neurotic or perverse. Neurotic characters had high defensive inhibitions that stifled drives and distorted emotional derivatives. In contrast, perverts had strong drives that were displaced rather than inhibited. That led to socially inappropriate actions such as voyeurism, exhibitionism, pederasty, sodomy, fetishism, sadism, and masochism (Abraham, 1924; Fenichel, 1945; Freud, 1923).

Freud conceptualized character pathology as the result of fixation at early levels of development of the libido (sexual energy) at oral, anal, or genital levels. This led to Freud's structural theory that a superego kept an id (source of raw libidinal and aggressive drives) in check by its influence on the organizing properties of an ego. In a perverse character, the superego was too weak in relation to the id. In a neurotic character, the superego was too strong or rigid in relation to the id. In both, the ego remained underdeveloped in skills of mastery of diverse pressures; therefore, ego ideals were not met. The failure to reconcile the id, ego, and superego could result in shame as a vital characterological emotion (Kohut, 1972, 1977; Wurmser, 1981).

Freud (1908) composed a paper defining a cluster of co-occurring traits as anal character. The paper became a classic. It seemed to support his hypothesis of an oral, anal, and genital progression of libidinal energy. As noted elsewhere, these oral/anal/phallic psychosexual classification theories are largely but not completely outmoded (Bowlby, 1969; Colarusso & Nemeroff, 1981; Emde, 1981, 1983; Kernberg, 1992; Pine, 1985; Stern, 1985). Instead, relational theories have evolved (Fairbairn, 1952, 1954; Guntrip, 1961, 1971; Kernberg, 1984; Klein, 1948; Ogden, 1992).

Relational theories led to person schemas theory (Bowlby, 1969; Horowitz, 1979, 1988, 1991; Jacobson, 1964; Knapp, 1991; Singer & Salovey, 1991; Stinson & Palmer, 1991). Role-relationship models are used as a way to formulate often unconscious self–other organizations. These organizational units are infused by inner motives as ways toward a desired end or away from a feared outcome. Instincts and drives may provide inner motives; passions are directed by the activated person schemas. Drivenness is not divided into just sex and aggression, but is enlarged to include ambitions for growth, self-coherence, and affiliations to others of various sorts.

CONFIGURATIONS OF FORM AND CONTENT

Belief structures such as person schemas have both form and content. *Form* has to do with the connectivity between meanings. Are there few or many linking associations? The answer will say something about the integrations of meanings. Many links are usually preferable, provided that they are not too irrational. *Content* has to do with the meanings that are inscribed as cognitive maps. The question asked about content might be What are beliefs about the self and others? What are recurrent aims, intentions, scripts, and plans of action? Psychotherapy for character development aims at change in both content and form in a belief structure.

A person can have many discordant meanings in the contents of person schemas or memory traces. This high degree of contradiction between beliefs could lead to conflict, but associational linkages and supraordinate schemas help integrate the antitheses of these meanings. These known connections can soften ambivalence about contradictions and help a person see conflicts as an expected rather than a demoralizing aspect of life.

Studies of successfully treated cases indicate that one source of enhanced character development is formation of a larger system of meanings (Horowitz, Kernberg, & Weinschel, 1993; Wallerstein, 1986). Through development of new supraordinate schemas, previously conflictual configurations are harmonized. In other words, integration of personal meanings into supraordinate schemas allows the person to balance self and relationship issues, and to maintain long-range intentions, values, commitments, and responsibilities. The person is then more aware of how love and hate occur in the same affiliation. The person can restrain selfish impulses and endure frustrations without rupturing a union.

WELL-DEVELOPED CHARACTER

Character becomes more complex and coherent as a person both learns and integrates multiple schemas. People with well-developed character have formed supraordinate schemas that integrate many associations. In well-modulated states of reflective consciousness, the person with a well-developed character knows that he or she has various states of mind and can anticipate going through a mood cycle. This well-developed person can tolerate periods of ambivalence between self and other without impulsive estrangement.

The person has an expectation of state variation in the other person and can tolerate shifts in warmth and coldness, closeness and distance, empathy and misunderstanding. Insults do not lead to enduring revenge fantasies. Warm episodes do not lead to expectations of all needs being fulfilled. Love may ebb and flow, but it seldom turns into hate. Well-modulated restraints, renunciations, sublimations, and rational choices occur. What must be accepted is accepted with wisdom and humor. The person can be emotionally influenced and deeply empathic, can share we-ness experiences without fear of loss of identity (Renick, 1990).

LEVELS OF PSYCHOPATHOLOGY OF CHARACTER

The well-developed character can be contrasted with neurotic, narcissistic, and borderline levels of character pathology. This is done by inferring, from the study of a person or typology, the level of integration of person schemas. Patterns noted in repeated stories involving the self and others are the source of such inferences. Table 7.1 gives definitions of several levels organized by descending levels of character pathology (Horowitz, 1990; Horowitz, Marmar, Weiss, DeWitt, & Rosenbaum, 1984).

NEUROTIC PSYCHOPATHOLOGY

Neurotic people usually manifest enduring conflicts in relationships; in psychotherapy, they manifest these conflicts in transference reactions. But they are also capable of seeing the therapist as a kind of teacher and the self as a kind of student. These roles represent an improvement from prior maladaptive role-relationship models. This change provides a first alliance for treatment; from this vantage point, insight may be gained. However, the person still has states organized for more regressive, less situationally appropriate transference reactions. These less adaptive transference reactions have negative emotional consequences: They are based on conflictual role-relationship model (RRM) configurations.

In challenging encounters with other people, neurotics often feel unsafe. They may lose the capacity to reason about their choices, and they repeat transference reactions that are inappropriate. Therapy can provide a safe relationship, and an alliance of trust that allows repeated examination of why certain challenges are so stressful.

In a safe relationship, despite conflict, neurotic persons can develop harmonious configurations. First, they can heighten awareness, which enables them to form a working model based on real properties of the current situation. Second, they can compare their less-adaptive transference reactions to their more-adaptive working model because they are capable of containing both views in reflective consciousness. Third, they can learn to form new connections between the various role-relationship models of a conflictual configuration.

By repetitions of awareness, the reasons for transference reactions are clarified. The person might then make new choices and engage in

TABLE 7.1
Psychopathology Defined by
Organizational Level of Person Schematization

Level	Description
Well Developed	These persons have a well-developed supraordinate self (a large schema containing several self schemas) and function from a relatively unitary position of self as having a hierarchy of values. When they have conflicts and negative moods, they own these as "of the self." Conflicts are between various realistic pros and cons about identity and relationships and are lived through by use of well-modulated actions, restraints, renunciations, sublimations, choices, wisdom, humor, or resignation. These persons know that another person is separate with equivalent characteristics of his or her own, also experiencing wishes, fears, emotional reactions, and conflicts. They organize interpersonal transactions and perceptions by usually harmonious configurations of RRMs.
Neurotic	These persons have long-standing, unresolved, and irrational themes of conflict. These contain antitheses and contradictions of intentions, expectations, and values. Defensive styles ward off emotional flooding but impair chances to reduce contradictions in identity and relationships. Discrepancies between views of self as agent of action and self as critic of action are not resolved by rational choices. They may see themselves continually as both intending to express some aim in behavior and opposing such expression on moral grounds. Repetitive maladaptive relationship cycles occur, which enact conflicts about autonomy of self, sexuality, and power. They organize recurrent but maladaptive interpersonal patterns according to conflicted configurations of role relationship models. They have both conflicted and harmonious supraordinate schematizations.
Narcissistically Vulnerable	These persons have frequent or intense states when they are vulnerable to feeling self-impoverished or grandiose. With further stress, they may lose a sense of

TABLE 7.1 (*Continued*)
PSYCHOPATHOLOGY DEFINED BY
ORGANIZATIONAL LEVEL OF PERSON SCHEMATIZATION

Level	Description
	self-cohesion. Grandiose, inferior, and realistic RRMs lead to states lacking in a sense of relationship continuity. Rigid compromises may impair reasonable self appraisal but stabilize mood. Grandiose delusions confined to a sphere such as creativity or sexuality might occur. Rage or narcissistic injury is frequent, yet the person may disown personal aggressive behavior that is flagrantly obvious to others. Such people often view others as mere extensions of self (self-objects). They externalize most blame onto others. They have conflicted configurations of self schemas and their RRMs contain unemphatic views of others. Supraordinate schemas fail to contain antitheses of realistic, degraded, and grandiose views.
Borderline	These persons are not able to stabilize a self-cohesion that includes positive and negative self-schemas within a supraordinate schema. Rather, they have various self-schemas that are each only part of the actual self, and various schemas of others that include only part of the actual behavior of others. Composites that are all good may be dissociated from composites that are all bad. Rage may be projected onto others and subtly provoked in others, intensifying the pattern of externalizing blame found in narcissistically vulnerable people. They have difficulty in forming supraordinate configurations of RRMs.
Fragmented	These persons have a self and other differentiation that is only partial and transitory. At times, they display or experience a significant level of confusion of self with other, or they regard self and other as merged or interchangeable. Parts of the bodily self may be disowned or dissociated. Psychotic states with grossly irrational beliefs occur when under stress. They are impoverished by a lack of supraordinate person schemas and by a fragmentation of subordinate schemas.

a trial of new patterns of behavior. Repetition of new behaviors leads to new schemas and to more harmonious configurations within supraordinate schemas.

NARCISSISTIC PSYCHOPATHOLOGY

Narcissistic persons have all the problems of neurotic characterization, and more, because they are so vulnerable to criticism of their identity. They activate a grandiose compensation to prevent a dreaded state of degradation. They have less supraordinate schematization of self. When threatened by anticipated worthless, degraded, and inferior self-concepts, they use an unrealistic inflation of self, while concurrently devaluing others and externalizing blame (Kohut, 1971, 1977). As Kohut observed, they also use others as self-objects (1971). The other serves as a mirror, idealizing the self as an admired figure, a great asset to supplement personal deficiency, or a twin to whom the self adheres for heightened power. Self-objects protect the self from states of shame, and they lift pride.

Narcissistically vulnerable persons usually start psychotherapy when an illusion of self-sufficiency falters (Modell, 1975). They then bolster the self by using the therapist as a self-object. The process of change usually must proceed at a slower rate than in neurotic-level patients. The narcissistically vulnerable patient can only gradually learn to develop a more realistic therapeutic alliance. A focus on the here and now and the immediate future helps in this process. Techniques for the neurotic patient, used too early with narcissistic or more disturbed patients, may be unhelpful; they may evoke under-modulated states of mind and distort defensive control processes (Loewald, 1957; Stone, 1954; Zetzel, 1970).

BORDERLINE PSYCHOPATHOLOGY

Persons at the borderline level of self and other schematization may split schemas into all good and all bad clusters of connected associations because this oscillation is preferable to chaos. (Greenberg & Mitchell, 1983; Kernberg, 1969, 1976, 1984, 1992; Ogden, 1992). When the other is appraised as bad, the good recognized in alternative states is absent. Others may even be dehumanized and regarded as monsters that should be destroyed, or glorified without regard for the truth. With such extreme beliefs, emotions become more intense, and irrational and impulsive actions are more likely.

The self may also be demonized or glorified. Instead of experiencing a sense of falling apart altogether—which could occur in anticipation of abandonment or when flooded with diffuse rage or panic—some people maintain their sense of cohesion by the irrational restoration of a whole as altogether good or altogether evil.

FRAGMENTED PSYCHOPATHOLOGY

Persons who remain at a fragmented level of self and other schematization are vulnerable when feeling abandoned, trapped, or helpless; unbearably intense emotions occur and break through the tenuous defensive control processes. Entry into psychotic states periodically occurs, organized only by chaotic fragments of identity. Then extreme defenses are used to create a more stable state of mind, one that presents grandiose and persecutory delusions. Unfortunately, these extreme restitutional efforts grossly distort appraisals of relationship opportunities, alienate others, and lead into a vicious circle of demoralization.

DEVELOPMENT

Character development emerges from the establishment of balance between what one sees as self-interest and one's relationship with others. Conflicts between aims for personal growth and aims for advancing others can be resolved by supraordinate schemas. The self can be empowered without self-aggrandizement that would demean others, and without abnegations that demean self. Cooperation and competition can balance, to everyone's benefit.

In character pathology, harmony has not been achieved. Instead, the person displays excessive self-aggrandizement or self-abnegation. Impulsive actions based on immediate desire and intolerance of frustration occur with no regard for probable social losses in the future.

Humans are characteristically social animals and most are quite concerned with self-enhancement and affiliation with others. This is reflected in the attention to the issues of virtue and vice in most societies. In lay psychology, social endorsements of a person's character often use words for virtues that are not excessively self-centered: mercy, forgiveness, fairness, wisdom, endurance, empathy, compassion, courage, fortitude, patience, humor, and temperance (Erikson, 1982). Because religious beliefs ascribe high value to social virtues, the opposite character traits have been socially certified as bad; they are called vices in some cultures. For example, such selfish traits as greed, gluttony, sloth, envy, anger, pride, and lust are called the seven deadly sins.

INFANCY AND EARLY CHILDHOOD

Table 7.2 presents a sequence of development in character structure. In the earliest developments, an inchoate sense of affiliation and union arises between the baby and its first beloved caretaker. Affiliative relationship schemas organize behaviors that Bowlby (1973) described as indices of secure attachment. That is, the infant develops precursors of traits of vitality, trust, and hope that result in a widening of positive affiliations to the group. Otherwise, negative traits of suspicion, rage, detachment, and despair may result (Ainsworth, 1973; Bretherton, 1985; M. Klein, 1948; Main, 1975; Sperling & Berman, 1994; Sroufe, 1979).

A successful infancy includes a secure attachment to at least one important caregiver, establishing a core basis of trust. The child forms self-confidence and a more differentiated understanding of others. Or, in strained situations, where security is absent or intermittent, fear of separation, doubt, and apathy could provide an early basis for a lifetime of anxious self-preoccupation. Various erroneous beliefs, especially concepts of self as worthless, might be inscribed, leading to a future pattern of systematically misunderstanding both one's own capacities and the intentions of others.

MIDDLE CHILDHOOD

Later on, a trusting and confident child can learn age appropriate self-restraint so as to fit in well with social customs. Under strain, the child's impulsive episodes of selfishness can lead to acts that violate social rules, which can lead to a basis for future antisocial patterns. A greater problem is that the vulnerability of children can make them a target of abuses and violations of social rules. Such violations usually involve adults who displace their rage or misplace their erotic im-

TABLE 7.2
LIFE THEMES AND DEVELOPMENT OF CHARACTER

Period	Personal Tasks and Social Expectations	Character
1. Infancy	Achievement attunement and secure attachments to other people; learn to walk and talk; acquire self-regulation	First expectations of others that lead to vitality, trust, and hope (versus rage, detachment, or despair)
2. Early Childhood	Increase bodily control; develop sense of right and wrong; learn communication skills; learn to negotiate; develop capacity for play and imagination; connect gender beliefs	Beliefs that lead to confidence and empathy for others (versus inaction or self-preoccupation)
3. Middle Childhood	Experiment with sensuality; relate to peers; form close friendships; learn to work on one's own; enlarge sense of morality	Self-restraint in relation to the rules of social contexts (versus impulsive selfishness)
4. Early Adolescence	Accept one's changing body; experiment with love and sexuality; forge peer groups; develop work and recreational abilities; differentiate ideal and real social practices	Apt value choices in social dilemmas (versus conformity or authoritarianism)
5. Late Adolescence	Improve modulation of emotion; extend understanding of gender and sexual roles; develop specific skills; learn to balance cooperation and independence	Intentions that preserve objectives (versus transient commitments)
6. Young Adulthood	Relate self to social systems of work and new families or groups	Responsibility for others (versus ruthlessness or self-abnegation)
7. Middle Adulthood	Accept bodily declines; give to older and younger generation; transmit skills	Appropriate use of power (versus excesses or paralysis)
8. Late Adulthood	Accept aged body; adapt to retirement; confront transience; pass on leadership; transmit values	Flexibility in relinquishing control with faith that values will survive personal death (versus sense of failure)

pulses. Such aggressions, especially if concealed between a social veneer of appropriate care, tend to damage self and relationship schemas, as already discussed.

Abuse builds contradictions of value within the child. The child expects adult protection, and now learns adult exploitation and disdain for the right to be a child.

The child is often puzzled by parental abuse, and does not take in only a simple, if horrible, role as victim. The child tries to figure out causes, and reasoning may lead to self blame. An abusing father might attribute blame to his daughter by saying "you should not have flirted with me." The daughter might blame herself. At the same time, she might inhibit contemplation so that contradictions are recorded as antitheses rather than being resolved into more apt conclusions. In the extreme, some instances of adult prostitution may be the result of such abuse. It portrays both the prostitute and the exploiting customer as "bad" in shifting ways.

Such schematic ideas are recorded without clear, conceptual awareness. That is why, in a treatment such as exploratory psychotherapy or psychoanalysis, the pattern is first clarified from stories about behavioral repetitions; and observations of the unconscious meanings are then interpreted. For example, a daughter who is repeatedly hit in the face when the parent was angry not only learns the role of victim but also the role of aggressor. She may vow to never be like her abusive parent, but as a mother, the frustrations that occur may activate impulses to strike her own child just as she was hit.

ADOLESCENCE

As the child moves out of the parental orbit, new experiences can lead to reschematization. Identity and relationship schemas are broadened, based on a great deal of bodily change and social experimentation that involves not only sexuality, but other group processes. Trials of new affiliations, alliances, and betrayal of alliances take place (Blos, 1979; Brody, 1992).

While experimenting with individuation and possibilities for social status, many adolescents attach themselves to social groups and cultural or anticultural role models. This can be both growth promoting and dangerous. A trial of antisocial acts may occur and then abate. Cultural rituals show the developing adolescent the balance point between freedom and responsibility.

The prerequisities of social status and the perils of transgressions are drawn into cognitive maps. Character begins to solidify as plans develop for handling these challenges and dilemmas. At this point, negative schemas can form. The adolescent may conform excessively, become dictatorial, or choose an eccentric path through the maze of available community roles.

In this structure of smaller systems of meaning, which are combined and integrated into larger systems and then form generalized beliefs, the late adolescent begins to weave a tapestry of values, intentions, and future plans. Sustained commitments can be established. Preservation of goals and rules for justice can be observed in those who are moving toward a well-developed character.

YOUNG ADULTHOOD

The young adult adds both new schemas of self and other and more supraordinate schemas to integrate them. Love is explored as a mutual relationship, possibly resulting in marriage. Work roles are examined, commitments are revised, and social status is gained or lost. As higher status is gained, and as power and perhaps wealth are accrued, the possibility for corruption of character increases. Responsibility for self and others is practiced as the alternative to either ruthless self-aggrandizement or self-impairing abnegations.

MIDDLE ADULTHOOD

By middle age, some people have gained control over others. Yet some of their ambitions, hopes, and cherished goals may have been disappointing; life is imperfect even for successful people. While meeting ongoing challenges, mature people usually continue to develop, learn flexible and appropriate uses of power, and accept personal limits. A person with a less well-developed character may resort to excessive use of power in order to be seen as powerful and great (Vaillant, 1993) as a compensation for a dreaded aging process, lack of self-esteem, or fragility of identity or coherence. Those who have excessive worries about bodily changes and doubts about competence and self-worth may succumb to a paralysis of action.

TABLE 7.3

LIFE THEMES AND THE FORMATION OF PERSONAL AND SOCIAL MEANING

Period	Personal Tasks and Social Expectations	Identity	Relationships	Character
1. Infancy	Achieve attunement and secure attachments to other people; elicit affection; learn to walk and talk; acquire self-regulation	First beliefs about self (versus fragmented ideas)	First understanding of self with other (versus lack of self-regulation because of lack of regulation by other)	First expectations of others that lead to vitality, trust, and hope (versus rage, detachment, or despair)
2. Early Childhood	Increase bodily control; develop sense of right and wrong; learn communication skills; learn to negotiate; develop play and imagination; connect gender beliefs	Sense of competence of self; gender identification; beliefs about various possible selves (versus incompetence)	Roles for emotional interactions (versus deficits and conflicts)	Beliefs that lead to confidence and empathy for others (versus inaction or self-preoccupation)
3. Middle Childhood	Experiment with sensuality; relate to peers; form close friendships; learn to work on one's own; enlarge sense of morality	Multiple self schemas and flexible shifts between them (versus rigidity and self doubt)	Multiple role relationship models of friendship, and rank; practices for leading, following, and doing work (versus apathy, or stigmatization)	Self-restraint in relation to the rules of social contexts (versus impulsive selfishness)
4. Early Adolescence	Accept one's changing body; experiment with love and sexuality; forge peer groups; develop work and recreational abilities; differentiate ideal and real social practices	More self schemas and resilient use of multiple self schemas (versus identity diffusion)	Resilient use of alternative roles and scripts for sexuality, disputes, and commitments (versus relationship confusion)	Apt value choices in social dilemmas (versus conformity or authoritarianism)

Period	Personal Tasks and Social Expectations	Identity	Relationships	Character
5. Late Adolescence	Improve modulation of emotion; extend understanding of gender and sexual roles; develop specific skills for work and socialization; learn to balance cooperation and independence	Supraordinate self schemas (versus dissociations)	Supraordinate role relationship models (versus dissociations)	Intentions that preserve objectives (versus transient commitments)
6. Young Adulthood	Relate self to social systems of work and new families or groups	Harmonious configurations of self schemas (versus continued dissociations or conflictual configurations)	Harmonious supraordinate configurations of role relationship models (versus continued dissociations and conflicted configurations leading to maladaptive but repeated relationship cycles)	Responsibility for others (versus ruthlessness or self-abnegation)
7. Middle Adulthood	Accept bodily declines; give to older and younger generation; transmit skills	Self-organization and hierarchy of personal values (versus self-disgust)	Relationship cogwheelings (versus contradictory relationships with older and younger generations)	Appropriate use of power (versus excesses or paralysis)
8. Late Adulthood	Accept aged body; adapt to retirement; confront transience; pass on leadership; transmit values	Wisely reschematized self-organization (versus terror or rage at ending life)	Schemas of the future in which concepts of the self and of valued relationships survive personal death (versus bitterness)	Flexibility in relinquishing control with faith that values will survive personal death (versus sense of failure)

159

LATE ADULTHOOD

As the body declines, even people with well-developed characters and those who have been socially privileged by high status, face a time for relinquishing their power, control, and leadership. They can develop a faith that others they love, a good world, and their products and values will persist after self death. This sense of leaving a legacy can lead to more serenity than bitterness. A sense of continuing integrity is maintained, or else despair over dying may occur (Erikson, 1950, 1958, 1959, 1970).

This sequence of development of character is shown in Table 7.2, using the same epochs of personal tasks and social expectations as in the prior chapters on identity and relationship development. The concept that character integrates both identity and relationship issues into a larger whole is illustrated by putting together the prior tables. The result is Table 7.3.

BALANCE AND IMBALANCE

Although genetically determined temperaments contribute to character traits, character is most heavily influenced by culture, society, and families. These groups place requirements on their members; they pressure new members to conform with pre-existing roles. The emerging self, the somatic drives, and social pressures mingle to influence character formation. The blend of these forces forms a very complex structure and leads to a balanced or an unbalanced cognitive map of values. Imbalance often tilts character toward either an excessive focus on self or an excessive focus only on the interests of others. Such imbalances can be manifested by a person discussing traits of self-aggrandizement and self-abnegation.

SELF-AGGRANDIZEMENT

If a parent worships a child regardless of bad behavior, then the child may lack adequate cues about his or her status in life, and may grow to believe in his or her own perfection. The child may behave as if the parent figure was an extension of self, not a separate being with autonomous wants and feelings. The child, even though hostile in demeanor, may develop a self-concept of being wonderously adorable, always expecting to receive total admiration from a devoted extension of the self.

Life plans develop; they include enduring expectations of total services from slave-like admirers. These admirers and caretakers are expected to read the mind of the dictator self, to mirror back an
idealized image of "the great one" (Kohut, 1972).

When such a child begins to interact with others beyond the home,
views of the self as a future king or queen of the world are challenged. Most children then replace grand views with realistic self-
concepts. But some are so threatened by deflating events that they
maintain or further develop inferior self-concepts. To avoid entry
into degraded states, the child continues to display arrogant entitlement and makes hostile demands on others. Self-righteous rages
occur on frustration. Destructive actions, based on inner distortions
about the intentions of others, do not lead to guilt; others are viewed
as monsters who deserve severe punishment.

A prototype of a conflictual role configuration of a self-aggrandiz-
ing character follows. The person with this character type may desire
but be unable to maintain solid interpersonal relationships (Benjamin, 1991; S. Cooper, 1989; Kernberg, 1984). This desired RRM casts
a worthy self, with a wish for warmth, seeking loyalty, admiration,
or affection from excellent others. This desired RRM is rigidly linked,
in associational connections, to a dreaded RRM. The dreaded RRM
casts the self in an abused role of being deliberately betrayed by an
evil or exploitative other. The wish–fear dilemma resulting from this
linkage is that if one seeks warmth, one will be betrayed.

To get out of the dilemma of seeking warmth and fearing betrayal,
a problematic compromise RRM is activated. It identifies self as a vigilant, besieged person who expects problems and who, like a boxer,
counterpunches to ward off betrayal and hostility. The problematic
pattern produces hypervigilance to harmful and abrasive behaviors.

Sometimes the individual believes that he or she is unappreciated
by others and becomes embittered and aloof from the perceived ne-
glecters. Devaluation and depreciation of others is expressed in caus-
tic derision based on this quasi-adaptive RRM.

This configuration of an RRM, put into expressive form, contains
the following beliefs about identity and relationships: "If I trust anyone (the desired RRM), then I will be betrayed (the dreaded RRM),
because I was betrayed. Before, when I trusted my parents, they were
not totally devoted to me. So I must protect myself by counterpunch-
ing first (the problematic RRM), and by depreciating others while
minimizing my desire for them (the quasi-adaptive compromise

RRM)." The quasi-adaptive compromise RRM contains a belief that all good things are self-formed and self-owned. Arrogant excesses of self-entitlement result; self-aggrandizement occurs at the expense of others. Their resentment is then an excuse for further withdrawal from attention to and empathy for others. The withdrawal makes it difficult to achieve desired relationship patterns.

Self-Abnegation

Some people spend their whole lives repeating patterns premised on fundamental fear of abandonment. As Bowlby (1969) pointed out, the root of this excessive fear was premature loss of parental figures and/or inability to attach securely to available figures (perhaps for biological reasons). Some such people use self-abnegation as an appeal for attention. Ties to others are bondage rather than self-confident searches for warmth and solace, love and friendship (Cooper, 1992).

Without another person to reflect personal characteristics, people with such character problems may experience dreaded states of mind with a conscious loss of coherence in identity. These sensations enter awareness and the person imagines the self on the brink of annihilation. If attention from the other falters then loss of contact is anticipated, and problematic anxious states occur. Such people may abnegate self just to remain close to another. The other is watched, and what is seen or felt serves to support a fragile sense of identity.

In a desired RRM, a self-abnegating person might identify the self as a dependent but worthy child. The other person is viewed as a good, attentive caregiver. A dreaded RRM may be rigidly linked to this desired RRM, resulting in a wish–fear dilemma. In the dreaded RRM, the self is cast in a role that is needy but unworthy. Actions that express needs evoke a negligent response in a bad or unreliable caregiver. The self is expecting to be abandoned. The anticipated dreaded state of mind is one of helplessness, unrequited longing, and identity annihilation.

In such a character, the self feels that something must be done to hold the relationship together, even if the appeals used increase dependency and limit personal development of autonomy. Exhibiting a state of suffering and pining can provide a way of forging a desired relationship. A "poor little me" presentation can rest on a problematic compromise RRM as a partial way out of the wish–fear dilemma.

The *pathetic* state gets some attention from professional helpers; however, the attention is then experienced as too little and too brief. A state of *anxious vigilance* occurs wherein the person is excessively vigilant to see if (and when) the expected rejection will take place.

If any disfavor is in the air, state, of *obsequious deference* or *passive-aggressiveness* appear. Both are defenses against the dreaded state of *rage and despair* from abandonment. Both can work to sustain a relationship using a quasi-adaptive compromise RRM. Instead of exploring the world independently in a zestful way, such people tend toward surface passivity and buried hostility. The use of the quasi-adaptive RRM with the passive role for self usually allows others to dominate them. Instead of a firm resolution to live well, they drift or follow in a pattern of self-abnegation. Even though they are dependent they resent the other for being unable to fill insatiable needs. The clinging relationships endure but are unpleasant for both parties.

Another variation of self-abnegation identifies the self as an abandoned and debased waif, pining for a loved one who is unavailable. The person believes the caretaking figure may be here now but will soon become hopelessly gone. Compensatory life plans develop; character is shaped by these plans.

Frank

Frank was an accountant who specialized in working with financially insolvent firms. He protected clients who were near bankruptcy from financial death. He never abandoned them until they were saved. He gave up his own time—including hobbies, sports, vacations, and social pleasures—to rescue these firms. Then, without rest, he went on to find and rescue the next client in need.

Frank's childhood had been filled with fantasies and worries about impending abandonment. He disliked and felt cheated by his father. He had learned early in his life that his father had pressured his mother to have an abortion when she was pregnant with Frank. She refused, but did abort her next pregnancy and then became depressed. His father was belligerent and blamed Frank for preoccupying his mother. Feeling totally abandoned, Frank developed a variety of childhood phobias. Only by clinging to others could he feel less afraid, but this was rarely achieved. For years, Frank felt barely tolerated by his father and neglected by his mother.

Frank developed fantasies that his father and mother were not his real parents. He imagined they would die and his real, loving parents would rescue him. He gained an ability to entice teachers to rescue him. In adolescence, he used a boyish pathos to get girls to rouse him from his lethargy and sadness. His growing abilities led to more self-confidence. He reversed roles and boldly rescued people to secure their gratitude, commitment, and continuing attention.

As a young adult, Frank was able to turn on his charming, wooing, and winning state with women. He offered help in many areas. But after he won a woman, his mood turned sour. Despite her actual behavior, he expected the women to suddenly dislike and leave him. Either excitement in the relationship would die or he would start fearing her death. He would then leave her before she could leave him.

Frank sought treatment and in it developed a transference reaction. He believed that his therapist was depressed or sick with cancer. Frank had a belligerent, chip-on-the-shoulder attitude claiming that the therapist was unreliable. He relented when the therapist remained steadfast, calm, hopeful, and unthreatened. In reality, the therapist was healthy and dependable.

During his work in therapy, Frank recognized a role-relationship model in which he was a weak child, unprotected by a distant, belligerent, and psychologically absent parent. His career was an unconscious choice for an adaptive compensation. He derived faith in his own strength from his ability to rescue moribund business firms. He would provide good, careful attention, increasing their incomes. Yet he had a script that flipped from desired to dreaded role relationship models. Even if he saved a company or a woman in need, he expected loss.

This cycle with its wish-fear dilemma was enacted in transference reactions. Although the therapist was attentive and Frank made early rapid progress in a working alliance with the therapist, Frank began to misperceive the therapist's silences as lifeless. He viewed clarifying remarks and interpretations as criticism. He criticized or devalued the therapy. The therapist clarified Frank's feelings, expectations, and intentions and confronted him with his patterns of excessive self-abnegation. Gradually, Frank's life plan to save and rescue others was traced to his fundamental fear of abandonment and his imperative desires for any kind of affiliation. This realization fueled Frank's effort to change his behavioral pattern. He allowed himself to expect companions to stay with him as the therapist had stayed with him despite his criticism and threats.

SUMMARY

Social groups pass moral judgments about character. In contrast, clinicians are more concerned with appraising a person's advancement in developing supraordinate integrations of smaller systems of meaning about identity and relationships. In the neutral stance of the clinician, the relevant issue is degree of integration of beliefs and values. Integration of beliefs and values means that intentions, expectations, commitments, and rules are schematized into priorities. The person can choose, to pursue the greater good. It is up to the patient, to determine these priorities; it is not for the therapist to impose his or her personal judgment. Having an automatic knowledge of priorities helps decision making occur more quickly so that choices can be made in hard situations. If commitment is more important than instant gratification, then impulsive wishes for immediate satisfaction are restrained.

Hard situations can, as in many stories, build character. Personal growth occurs if challenges are well met. A well-developed character can live through strife with courage and resilience; the same turbulence in a less well-developed character can lead to explosive shifts in state, impulsive and wrong decisions, or indecisiveness, demoralization, and debasement.

Growth in character in the midst of life challenges involves the development of supraordinate schemas. These contain apt configurations of form and content. They depict models of how one should handle dilemmas and act for the benefit of both self and others. Aristotle said that happiness is a sense of slow growth. Perhaps he meant growth in character.

CHAPTER 8

Character Integration during Psychotherapy

MANY PSYCHOTHERAPIES aim only at symptom reduction. Others aim at both symptom reduction and character development. When better integration of character is a goal, therapists emphasize techniques that help patients heighten conscious awareness of the discrepancy between real opportunities and repetitive maladaptive patterns. Therapists also provide a safe relationship, a haven for an often emotional contemplation of possible new life plans; previously unspeakable, unthinkable topics are clarified, and the person gains new insights. Therapists then help patients make new decisions about how to modify person schemas that are based on irrational beliefs. Prior configurations of conflicted role-relationship models (RRMs) can become more harmonious, and new patterns of behavior can replace defensive avoidances of wish–fear dilemmas.

The hard and slow work of change requires time and a secure place. The priority is to increase the stability of working states. Labeling one's desired and dreaded states of mind increases awareness, conscious control, and therapeutic communication. The therapist helps the patient note when trigger stimuli lead to shifts in state, especially into undermodulated states. As the danger of emotional flooding is reduced, defenses can be lowered and the patient can afford to gain awareness into the reasons for recurrent state cycles (Gray, 1994; Sandler & Sandler, 1984). Maladaptive cycles can be anticipated and some can be stopped before they reach dreaded states.

The opposite is also true: With increased safety, some patients increase defensiveness to avoid further emotional turbulence. Overmodulated states during therapy sessions can increase rather than decrease. This can be a time for therapists to teach additional awareness skills such as free association, speaking what comes to mind, analyzing fantasies, and concentrating on the intentions that lie behind behaviors. Words are used to translate bodily and sensory expressions into clear statements. Sometimes, explorations of dreams and daydreams, or creative products such as art works are used to investigate symbolic condensations. The therapist then helps the patient differentiate between realities and fantasies.

The therapist refocuses the patient when derailment of dialogue takes place. When the patient says "I don't know" or declares a topic too difficult or unimportant, the therapist stays on the topic and explains why avoidance behaviors occur. As the dialogue resumes, the therapist helps the patient attend to the emotional heart of conflicted topics.

The patient learns to think about intentions: What motivates the self, what does the self expect, and what do others expect and intend? This helps the patient understand how social life is a play of competing and cooperating motives. Now the patient can examine the interaction and balance between passions and values, freedoms and constraints.

Modifying habitual avoidances and distortions enables a patient to handle conflictual themes in the present and future. By modifying his or her defenses, a patient can acquire new cognitive and emotional skills. The therapist facilitates this development by teaching attention control. *Clarifications* identify what happened in a cause and effect sequence of a specific story. *Confrontations* challenge the patient's specific avoidances. Clarifications, and sometimes confrontations, point the patient's awareness towards usually obscure themes. *Interpretations* tell the patient how themes are connected with related topics, why they recurr, and when mental contents that were once unthinkable can be contemplated.

In addition to clarification, confrontation, and interpretation, the therapist fosters *learning*. Learning occurs declaratively, from new facts, and procedurally as from identification with role models. By copying the therapist's calm but clear communicative style, the patient is able to speak more amply about emotional topics. The patient learns to use reflective conscious thought to make apt choices. Gradually, wish–fear dilemmas are solved directly without habitual use of compromised RRMs. The patient repeats actions based on new decisions, and this repetition helps forge a reschematization of RRMs.

The patient makes new decisions to build skills in the future, takes the necessary risks of living more boldly, and mourns idealized goals that can never be realized. Self-criticism becomes less irrationally harsh. More empathy for others occurs, and urges are harmonized with values. In these new practices the patient is bolstered by a more coherent sense of identity and an increase in both self-esteem and compassion. Relationship ties are maintained responsibly. An increase in affectionate commitments, receiving and giving friendship, and rewards for work and care of others, reinforce the gains in knowledge and personal power.

Termination is an important part of the therapeutic process. The end of therapy often involves mourning goals of perfection not attained and the transience of relationships. Some conflictual relationships are not fully resolvable, and such situations become accepted as troublesome companions. The patient learns how to live with inevitable problems without entry into dreaded states. The modification of defenses and enhanced self-observational skills put the patient in a position to go on changing throughout life.

THERAPEUTIC ALLIANCE

A patient beginning psychotherapy forms a *therapeutic alliance* based on a working model of a relatively appropriate relationship with the therapist (Greenson, 1967; Luborsky & Crits-Christoph, 1990; Strupp & Binder, 1984; Zetzl, 1970). The therapeutic alliance differs from *social alliances* that have social roles for give and take by both parties, and *transference alliances* that contain relatively unrealistic expectations (Horowitz, 1987; Horowitz, Marmar, Krupnick, et al., 1984). Each therapist–patient pair forms a unique therapeutic alliance. A prototype of such an RRM is provided in Figure 8.1.

Observations of the real communicative and supportive opportunities in therapy revise this initial working model; gradually the working model is transformed to better fit the present situation. As the initial therapeutic alliance is changed, a reschematization of relevant RRMs occurs.

Freud (1912, 1915) at first focused treatment on the recollection of repressed traumatic events. Then he discovered the importance of

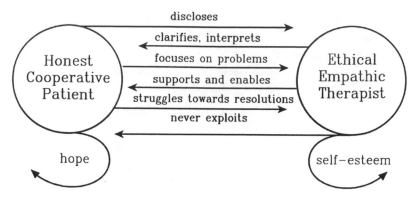

FIGURE 8.1
AN RRM OF A THERAPEUTIC ALLIANCE

analyzing transference and resistance. Later analysts (Aron, 1996; Greenberg and Mitchell, 1983; Greenson, 1967; Horowitz, Kernberg and Weinschel, 1993) focused on character development and the importance of a gradually developing alliance. Techniques focused on helping the patient discover the historical basis of transference roles for self and other and how these differed from the roles of the therapeutic alliance. Interpreting the causes of resistance and transference reactions became the core of psychoanalysis, and the goal was reduction of irrational interpersonal behaviors in the future.

Emotionally intense transference states occur when warded-off relationship models are primed by memories and fantasies about the therapist. Some modification of defensive control processes has to occur before it is safe to develop such regressive reactions. The patient often tests the therapeutic alliance for safety before reducing defensiveness (J. Weiss, 1993; J. Weiss & Sampson, 1986). This interaction of defensive modification with reschematization is illustrated in Figure 8.2.

Figure 8.2 illustrates a movement of reschematization from primitive to well developed. Primitive schemas are mainly formed in childhood. The modification of person schemas does not erase such RRMs; they remain and can activate regressive states. Such states are less likely to occur, however, because mature supraordinate schemas keep primitive schemas from operating inappropriately.

Figure 8.2 shows how a therapeutic alliance can emerge even in the context of transference and counter-transference provocation. As safety is built, warding-off operations are reduced. But if the therapist develops a countertransference and behaves unreliably, manip-

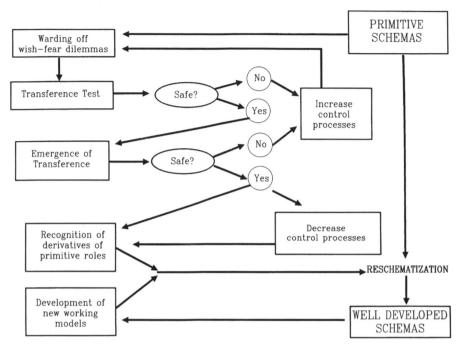

FIGURE 8.2
CONTROLS AND SCHEMAS

ulatively, or abusively, the patient feels endangered. Of course, even if the therapist is ethical and well trained, he or she will sometimes respond unwittingly to provocations. Responses of irritation, criticism, or inappropriate interpretations occur, perhaps in subtle guises. Then the patient may transiently appraise the situation as nontherapeutic and unsafe. Due to danger, the patient increases control processes to prevent entry into dreaded states.

The alert therapist can recognize shifts into defensive states, as the patient increases use of control processes. The therapist infers why this happened, looking for both transference and countertransference enactions. Accurate interpretation at this point can reduce the sense of danger and the defensive consequences.

In the conditions of safety provided by accurate interpretations and a therapeutic alliance, the patient can develop an awareness of primitive roles, transactional expectations, and insight into how irrational beliefs developed. A comparison of new working models and primitive roles occurs in reflective consciousness. It leads to new, more rational decisions. The patient then practices new behaviors that are more adaptive and less dysfunctional, and that provide a rewarding increase in social satisfaction. The repetition of adaptive behavioral patterns establishes new schemas and new connections between schemas. Supraordinate schemas form and provide a greater resiliency for adaptation to future stressors in life (Horowitz, 1992; Loewald, 1957; Stone, 1954; Weiss & Sampson, 1986).

Some of these interactions between reduction in defensiveness and reschematization processes are illustrated in the cases of Shirley and Hank. In both cases, unconscious schemas for emotional control were partially counteracted by a safe, therapeutic alliance and a new, conscious deployment of attention. Less defensiveness and more focused attention led to increased awareness. Repeated episodes of new awareness led to more insight, which in turn led to new plans for action and better relationship consequences. Each improvement increased a sense of security and led to satisfactions that accelerated the processes of change.

For each case (of Shirley and Hank), a brief history is given, followed by a case formulation. The processes of character change through the integration of conscious and unconscious beliefs is then described. The key steps of each formulation are based on the foundation of this book (as first outlined in Table 1.1, page thirty, in Chapter 1). This system of formulation is called *configurational analysis* (Horowitz, 1987, 1991a, 1997a). It describes phenomena, state cycles, habitual defenses, and person schemas. Enduring and conflictual beliefs are clarified using configurations of desired, dreaded, and compromised RRMs.

SHIRLEY

Shirley began psychotherapy at 30 years of age. She had symptoms of depression, agitation, and low self-esteem. The breakup of her relationship with her lover precipitated her motivation for therapy. Other breakups had occurred in the same way, so she felt defective and unlovable. In addition, she was drifting in her career choices, and conflicts emerged in her relationships with her friends.

FORMULATION

A formulation of her problems was derived from stories about her past developmental and current professional and intimate relationships, and observation of her verbal and nonverbal transactional signals in the clinical sessions. Using the configurational analysis method, Step 1 focuses on *problematic phenomena*. Shirley's symptoms consisted of periods of protracted depression, low self-esteem, and agitation.

Step 2 is a *state analysis*. Shirley's agitation was observed most prominently within a shimmering state of mind called *anxious tension*. In this state, she seemed like an uncertain adolescent who treated the therapist as a competent adult who would take charge of her situation. She was passive but also vigilant to what the therapist intended. She would both express herself and retreat from engaged communication.

When the therapist asked concrete questions and expected specific answers, Shirley had a shift in state. The shift was from the shimmering state of *anxious tension*, with its discordant signs of engaging the therapist and then retreating, to a disengaged state of *distracted cloudiness*, with eye movements to the ceiling and corners of the room, and slow, disjointed speech patterns. In this overmodulated state, Shirley was not agitated. Yet Shirley moved like an uncertain adolescent, not an adult woman. She seemed unaware of the therapist and was no longer hyperalert. Rather, she ignored the therapist and expected to be ignored, presenting emotionless small talk.

The shimmering state of *anxious tension* was formulated as a problematic compromise and the *distracted cloudiness* as a quasi-adaptive compromise because it did not contain agitation. These defensive states warded off a threatening, dreaded state of *agitated depression*, but they also prevented a desired state of *alert, working companionship*.

Step 3 of the configurational analysis focuses on *habitual styles of defensiveness*. Shirley frequently manifested her overmodulated state of *distracted cloudiness*. In other states, especially during her state of *anxious tension*, she inhibited emotional topics. When she approached a theme that bothered her, she prematurely closed discussion by saying, "I don't know." As she related stories about troublesome recent events, she could not reveal what actions caused other reactions. Even the sequences of events were poorly connected. It was as if she did not associate her response with what another person did. She did not think deeply about the intentions of others, and she missed cues in their behavior. If pressed for information, she entered a *distracted cloudiness* state.

Step 4 of this system for case formulation focuses on *person schemas*, as shown in Figure 8.3. Shirley hoped for mutual compe-

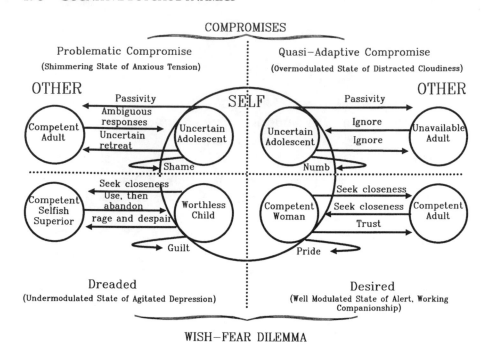

WISH–FEAR DILEMMA

FIGURE 8.3
A CONFLICTUAL RRM CONFIGURATION FOR SHIRLEY

tence and closeness with the people around her. Her future plan was to achieve companionship, friendship, and love; trust, pride, and self-esteem would then result. But early in treatment, Shirley believed that by seeking closeness, she might miss mutuality and achieve only abuse; therefore, the most observable state and role-relationship model was one of problematic compromise. During her shimmering states of *anxious tension* Shirley behaved like an uncertain adolescent who did not know what to expect nor how to act with a competent adult. She offered only a passive surface; she did not think much about the intentions and motives of the other person. She did not know if she should open herself to an encounter or retreat: Although she wanted closeness, she feared exploitation. She observed this behavior and felt shame at her own uncertainty and awkwardness.

Rather than experience tension and shame, Shirley, when she could, preferred to shift her state to *distracted cloudiness*. She felt ignored but less threatened by feared exploitation. She regarded herself as a passive and uncertain adolescent, who, because she was not an active woman, would not interest adults. They seemed unavailable and tended to ignore her as she ignored them.

Beneath the surface of the compromise RRM shown in Figure 8.3 was a wish–fear dilemma. Shirley dreaded the reenactment of a script that would put her in the role of a worthless and discarded child. Clarification of the desired and dreaded states and RRM exposed the more emotional components of her conflict.

The dreaded scenario would begin, as in her desired script, with her open search for closeness. Then a competent but selfish other would exploit her from a position of superiority without valuing her welfare. Once used, she expected abandonment and reacted with rage. She could rage at the other, but that would only prove her worthless. She would feel guilty, as if this rage caused her abandonment and would end in despair. To escape this danger it was preferable, although problematic, to shift into *anxious tension*.

The *anxious tension* state had symptoms. But these symptoms were not as bad as those in the state of *agitated depression*. In that state, perhaps because of combined mind-brain reasons, she could not rouse herself to reasoned activity, she felt herself drowning in a vast lake of painful feelings. Her retreat from others protected her. She felt safer in her state of *distracted cloudiness*. But the human instinct for affiliation made her lonely, and Shirley would once again seek closeness and the state of alert, working companionship. For a time, she could feel good, anticipating connection. Then she anticipated exploitation, and the cycle repeated itself.

CHANGE PROCESSES

In the course of treatment, the therapist helped Shirley gain awareness of usually warded-off themes by clarifying and labeling her feelings and somatic actions. Her vagueness about verbal labeling was initially countered by the therapist, who provided specific words. Later, he clarified the nature and motives for her defensive ambiguities and urged her to clarify meanings by herself. For example, in discussing her transition from states of erotic arousal to anxiety-filled tension states during sexual courtship, Shirley referred to all sexual body parts as "it" or "things." The therapist repeated what she had said, adding specific words for body parts. He pointed out her fear of being specific.

Shirley gradually became more aware of the occasions when she was vague and ambiguous. At such times, through identification with the therapist, she made a conscious effort to be clear, stay on a topic rather than end it short of insight, and make new decisions. She came to feel more and more comfortable speaking of the previously unthinkable matters of sexuality and hostility that her family had treated as unmentionables.

When Shirley started shifting from an alert, well-modulated working state into a distracted, cloudy state, the therapist would repeat what she had said. Hearing in his voice the words she had just uttered, she seemed startled and surprised. When he repeated what she had dreamily said, it seemed more real to her; when she spoke, it did not seem to count as a real idea. The therapist pointed out the way she experienced herself as an inauthentic sham of a woman rather than as a meaningful person who, as he believed deserved to speak her ideas and feelings.

Shirley enlarged her network of available associations. She began to understand cause-and-effect sequences. She asked herself about her own intentions and what she could realistically expect from her companions. She learned to think more clearly and plan her actions in advance.

At first, Shirley was startled when the therapist made a clarification or interpretation. She sometimes misinterpreted his intentions; she feared that she might enter a vulnerable state in which she could be exploited, manipulated, and hurt. She had heard about transference love for therapists and feared that he was evoking it. With insight into this fear of his manipulation, she was able to contrast that view with another view: She saw a relationship between a seeking patient and a helping expert who was neither manipulative, exploitative, nor sexually aroused. In addition, he would not abandon her or become cold and detached.

As Shirley developed the role-relationship model of a safe therapeutic alliance, she could spend more time in the *alert working* state organized by this schema. She thought of new solutions to interpersonal dilemmas and practiced them until they became more automatic.

Because Shirley felt more in control during these working states, she could allow herself to associate more fully, thus increasing her insight into when and why she felt strong emotions. She learned that she could tolerate strong emotions better if she did not shift into a state organized by defective self schemas; she could then think about conflicting ideas.

In recalling memories about her father, mother, and other child-hood figures, Shirley gained a clearer perspective on her develop-ment and beliefs about people. Memories once organized from a child's frame of reference were now reorganized into her adult con-text. She could review her past, see her repetitions, and know why they occurred. Although she had no memories of sexual abuse, she did recall episodes in which she felt seduced by inappropriate flirta-tions and play with certain adults. She alternated between feelings of excitement, depersonalization, and fear. She became aware of an irra-tional belief that only erotically appealing women could get atten-tion, and that she would be abandoned if she expected, from others, empathy to her own needs and feelings.

As Shirley moved from a passive to an active sense of identity, she decided to change her career to one that was more assertive and re-warding. She began to deliberately explore her own body and be-come more clearly aware of her bodily sensations. She developed self-concepts as an adult woman, rather than as an excited but en-dangered child. She decided that she was capable of an adult, ma-ture, and well-selected sexuality without harm.

Shirley began to enjoy her sexuality more and that in turn bol-stered her self-confidence and self-esteem. Increased boldness led to increased and clearer confrontations with her fears; she was able to make rational readjustments to them. Active, strong, and sexual self schemas were now available for use as organizers of her states of mind.

Shirley became more sagacious about the balance in her relation-ships. Her work creativity became more assertive because she was less tense when seeking attention. She was able to reduce contact with her intimate companions when work demands merited a tran-sient increase in time. She was also able to say no in an effective way to people at work when their demands interfered with important so-cial engagements.

The sense of a harmonious balance between different types of rela-tionships gave Shirley a sense of continuity, a future purpose in life, and a confidence in her ability to cope with challenges. Now that she no longer anticipated dire abandonment, she was better able to think about caring for others. She decided she wanted to have children in the future, and was able to balance this with her intentions to con-tinue to be effective in her field.

Shirley's character changes can be understood by examining the changes in her role relationship models (Figure 8.3). The desired relationship of closeness and trust between competent adults was the same both before and after treatment (Figures 8.3 and 8.4). This was more readily achieved as a state of *alert working companionship*. The dreaded relationship of being an abandoned, enraged, despairing, guilty, and worthless child was not erased. But it was diminished in activity so that her dreaded undermodulated state of *agitated depression* (as shown in Figure 8.3) seldom occurred. Instead, in the more harmonious role relationship model configuration shown in Figure 8.4, she dreaded a more acceptable, less overwhelmed state of *sorrow*. She retained a self-concept as a competent women who had sought closeness.

She viewed her aim for a deep relationship as appropriate. She viewed her intentions as admirable and her actions as capable. She regretted a break-up but recognized that the other person was too selfish to relate well with her and had instead merely dallied with her and then left. She felt frustration and sorrow, but did not experience, or expect to experience, the rage, despair, and guilt shown in the dreaded role relationship model before treatment. She did not revert to identity experiences organized by a worthless child self schema. Because this scenario for sorrow at the end of the relation-

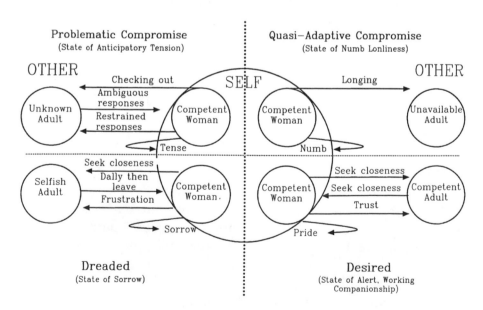

FIGURE 8.4

A MORE HARMONIOUS RRM CONFIGURATION FOR SHIRLEY

ship was not as catastrophic as the abandonment scenario, she no longer was in a wish–fear dilemma. She could attempt the desired state of closeness in a relationship because she knew she could withstand failure to achieve the desired degree of affiliation.

Modification of identity took place. Shirley reconfigured her self schemas so that the worthless child and uncertain adolescent roles were no longer viable patterns of associated beliefs about self. Her skills at work, her capacities for loving and befriending, her active goals for self-development, and her body image as a mature and attractive grown-up woman became the main features for a supraordinate sense of identity.

Communication about her positive attributes had established these realistic linkages. Communication about her negative fantasies of being immature, vulnerable, uncertain, passive, and incompetent were designated as preserved memories and imaginations of the past, not as current attributes of self. She could view herself as a lonely adult rather than an abandoned child, capable of going through a mourning process for separated relationships, and capable of developing other rewarding intimacies in the future. Unpleasant feelings would still occur in such dreaded states of the more harmonious configuration, but not overwhelming, undermodulated, and demoralizing ones.

Another shift in enduring beliefs occurred at the problematic compromise level. In comparing Figures 8.3 and 8.4, note that at the end of treatment Shirley still had states in which she expected others to behave in an ambiguous manner. They might become rewarding companions or not. Before treatment, she regarded herself as an uncertain adolescent behaving foolishly in a state of *anxious tension*. She ended up feeling shame because she did not know how to be engaged with a competent adult whom she could not understand. In contrast, after therapy, she had a state of *anticipatory tension* that was without shame. She viewed herself as a competent adult and the other as a person who was not yet well known. There was less shimmering between expressing and stifling emotions during this state of interpersonal uncertainty, as compared with equivalent social situational experiences before treatment. In this state of *anticipatory tension*, she retained identity experiences as a competent adult. She was clearer with new people, whom she felt uncertain about, as to her boundaries and expectations.

In a similar manner, there was a change in her quasi-adaptive compromise RRM. Shirley entered a state of *distracted cloudiness* less frequently. Instead, she could endure loneliness when that was necessary. She experienced a dull but acceptable placidity at such times. She called it *numb loneliness*. She felt like a competent adult who was alone; it was not what she desired, but it was tolerable.

HANK

Hank, a man in his mid-30s, sought psychotherapy for personality problems that included sexual difficulties and work inhibitions. In his intimate relationships, he was inconsistent; he was either too sexually aggressive and preoccupied with sexual fantasies, or too timid. At work, he misunderstood the intentions of others and was either too self-assertive or too passive. Earlier, during law school, his ability was marred by procrastination. Now, in a large law firm, his ambition to be promoted was thwarted by the fact that he could not make himself write complete briefs in a timely manner. This avoidance of completing work tasks was not joyful self-indulgence; it involved painful rumination. At work he might ruminate about his sexual life, and conversely, while with a woman, he might ruminate about work. Too frequently, he experienced premature ejaculation or could not stay erect when his partner was most excited.

FORMULATION

Hank's *symptomatic phenomena,* as described in Step 1 of configurational analysis for case formulation, included problems with cooperation; he was both excessively competitive and overly cooperative. His ineffectual performances were caused by a wavering intent. At key moments, he might shift from aggressive overassertiveness to unattractive obsequiousness.

In Step 2 of configurational analysis, his different *states* were described. Hank first presented a shimmering state of *anxious wavering*. He made firm, aggressive statements to the therapist about the help he wanted, but he quickly wavered into passivity, with a timid request that the therapist ask him leading questions. Hank then shifted into an even more overmodulated *obsequious* state of seeming acquiescence to whatever the therapist said.

As the therapist pointed out these state qualities, Hank spoke of how he desired to achieve a different state, one he seldom entered.

This desire was for a well-modulated state in which he could experience *victorious joy* from competing successfully. He dreaded that instead he would experience an intense and unbearably searing *remorse* at having defeated someone. Hank presented himself as weak in his *obsequious* state and strong in his momentary demands to totally lead the way and control what the therapist might do. The strong and weak gambits shimmered in a state of *anxious wavering*.

In Step 3 of a configurational analysis, the focus is on *defensiveness*. Hank's habitual defensive maneuvers were prominent during his shimmering state. He switched views about strength and weakness with such astonishing speed that his discourse was confusing. He might start a sentence speaking about himself as the strong competitor in a situation of seeking work advancement, beating a rival for the attention of a women or being a potent seducer of women, but by midsentence his adjectives reverted to speaking of himself as relatively weak. He might start to challenge the therapist's last remark, but would quickly submit to its undoubted correctness and pertinence. Even so, he did not focus on self-observation.

Step 4 formulates *person schematic beliefs*, which vary from state to state. Hank presented himself in antithetical roles as too weak and too strong in relation to others. His confusing oscillations between these extremes stemmed from developmental experiences in childhood and adolescence. Hank had feared that he would not develop enough strength to escape from his father. He feared that his father would always excessively dominate him. Staying closely united to his father meant that Hank would always remain the weaker party; he could never leave home and develop his own manhood. This became an irrational and pathogenic belief: He was desperate to escape but felt badly whenever he felt he was succeeding. He believed that to become strong and independent he would have to compete with and destroy his father to escape from his influence over him.

The father had been excessive in putting Hank down, or in depreciating his boyhood attempts at manly skill. In addition, as Hank became strong during adolescence, he seemed to humiliate rather than please his father. After the father developed a chronic and mildly debilitating illness, both Hank and his father shared irrational beliefs that the son's development of strength and skill had somehow diminished the father's strength. Hank felt guilty as a result and schematized the dreaded scenario in his wish–fear dilemma.

This scenario remained as an unconscious fantasy. That is why, in adult life, Hank sometimes reacted to senior lawyers in his firm as if he were showing up his sensitive and vulnerable father. His signaled attitude was inappropriate to the actual situation because he was dealing with people who were tough operators in an arena involving both cooperation and competition. Hank used weak self-concepts to undo the threat of strong self-concepts.

Hank's view, as a child, was that his father forced his mother to submit to vile sexual acts. Hank interpreted sounds he had heard from his parents' bedroom as his father's brutal and lust-ridden attack on her vulnerable and unwilling body. Hank feared being forced into a submissive role, like that which subjugated his mother. To avoid feeling weak, Hank cast himself into the role of a powerful, strong leader when he fantasized about his future life, or into a role as the male bull in a domineering sexual fantasy.

His childhood play and adolescent fantasies, as recalled during psychotherapy, contained themes in which he emerged victorious from deadly conflicts. In adulthood Hank tempered these themes, but he still viewed the law as combat, and sought admiration for displays of his skill when in competition with other lawyers. Preparing a subtle but incisive argument was his best way of showing off. Through such acts, he planned to gain status and surpass all others.

Hank could not enjoy the fruits of such a sequence of events, even in his adult daydreams. Embedded in this scenario was fear. When Hank reached the point where he was manifestly strong, he feared a response from others, as if his triumph had harmed them just as he had believed his father had harmed his mother. He would have to feel either guilty over their sufferings from defeat in competition or fearful of their retaliation, as in his problematic state of *anxious wavering*. He had to interrupt his daydreams when images reached this point in the scenario. He would then ruminate unpleasantly about how envious they would feel about his success or how he had to protect himself from their retaliatory aims. His efforts at avoiding the hazards of strength led to his *obsequious* state.

The desired and dreaded role-relationship models, in which he was the strong victor and another male (the defeated rival), was developed largely in the context of his internalized, partly real and partly fantasized relationship with his father. Hank had felt envious rage toward his father and wanted to become more powerful, more in control than his father. He also wanted to triumph without de-

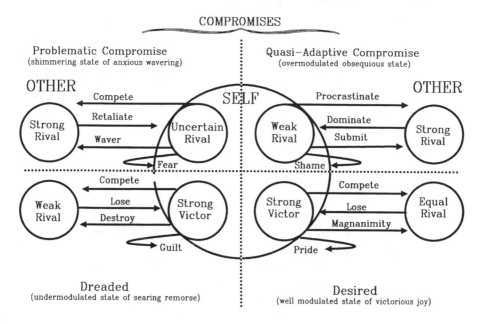

COMPROMISES

Problematic Compromise	Quasi–Adaptive Compromise
(shimmering state of anxious wavering)	(overmodulated obsequious state)

OTHER

SELF

OTHER

Compete — Strong Rival
Retaliate
Waver — Uncertain Rival
Fear

Procrastinate — Weak Rival
Dominate
Submit — Strong Rival
Shame

Compete — Weak Rival
Lose
Destroy — Strong Victor
Guilt

Compete — Strong Victor
Lose
Magnanimity — Equal Rival
Pride

Dreaded	Desired
(undermodulated state of searing remorse)	(well modulated state of victorious joy)

WISH–FEAR DILEMMA

FIGURE 8.5

A CONFLICTUAL RRM CONFIGURATION FOR HANK

stroying his father, and enter a state of *victorious joy*. But Hank sometimes fantasized about killing his father during his rage. This scenario led to the dreaded state of *searing remorse*. Some aspects of his wish–fear dilemma, and compromise RRMs are shown in Figure 8.5.

Hank could not find the right blend of teamwork in both cooperation and competition. That problem was enacted in his therapeutic alliance and transference during treatment. He had to learn that the therapist was not debasing him when he pointed out Hank's problematic behaviors and encouraged him to cooperate with a process of careful observation. The therapy itself helped Hank to integrate these themes in his character.

CHANGE PROCESSES

During psychotherapy, when he described himself as a powerful, incisive worker, Hank became anxious. He quickly began speaking as if he were submissive to the therapist's opinions. When he became anxious about his notion that the therapist always knew what was best, he would switch back to speaking of himself as powerful and in control.

A similar pattern occurred when Hank talked about his current sexual relationship. When describing how he had performed well sexually, he rapidly switched concepts. Instead of self as good and sexually powerful, the desired RRM, he switched from joy to a fear of being too powerful and potentially harming his partner, the dreaded RRM. Sometimes the switch was from his power to his weakness: He would shift to feeling dominated by her plans, desires, and needs, the quasi-adaptive compromise. He feared the shame of losing his independence.

Hank gained insight about repeatedly placing himself in a damned-if-he-did, damned-if-he-didn't dilemma involving his work and love life. He did not consciously recognize the entangled schemas that he rigidly imposed on life situations. He was not yet clear about his recurrent cycles. The next goals for his treatment were to become aware of these sequences and to make inferences about the schemas that led to each repetition.

Hank presented his ideas in a seemingly clear way, setting the stage for a story by describing the background, and then giving a sequence of events in great detail. But he ignored actions and emotions at the heart of the story; he progressed to more peripheral details. When the therapist confronted Hank with his pattern of avoiding the emotional and personal implications when telling a story, Hank responded by courteously agreeing, without changing his behavior.

Because the therapeutic alliance permitted safety even during challenging confrontations, the therapist became more persistent. Hank began to lose his courteous veneer and allowed himself to feel that the therapist was forcing him to conform to the therapist's own plan of how the treatment ought to proceed. At other times, Hank felt that he was beating the therapist down, harming him by ignoring the usefulness of his interpretations. He had difficulty comparing these beliefs with the concept that the therapist was neither dominating him nor submitting to him, neither rejoicing in molding him excessively nor feeling degraded and ineffectual that he could not cause any change in Hank.

Little by little, Hank came to see both himself and the therapist as having different roles, but on an equal footing in terms of dominance and submission. Against this standard of cooperation and trust,

Hank confronted the irrationality of his belief based on his pre-existing repertoire of RRMs. As he developed a new RRM of equivalent status with the therapist, his trust deepened, his cooperation increased, and his self-esteem grew.

Hank reduced the frequency of his defensive intellectualizations, rationalizations, and generalizations. He was able to acknowledge when he felt anxious and entered a momentary state of confusion, rather than having to gloss it over with his previous habitual mannerism of fast, bright talking. He could stop and try to tune up visual images that represented emotion and translate feelings into words.

As Hank learned to avoid use of his devious *obsequious* state, he found that his fears of entering too-strong states were excessive. He found that he did not have to enter dreaded states of uncontrolled rage and its consequence of *searing remorse* for excessive expressions of hostility. He learned to speak directly in an understandable, well-modulated, emotional way, even when he was talking about unpleasant topics.

His unconscious defenses had stifled emotion by rapidly switching topics and concepts. These excessive controls were now often set aside. Conscious efforts to go to the heart of a theme, facilitated by the attention-focusing maneuvers of the therapist, became more prevalent. He could change topics deliberately without putting down the therapist; he could stay on a topic initiated by the therapist without feeling subjugated, and he could disagree with the therapist and feel safe.

Meanwhile, at work, Hank began to recognize that equals might compete or even fight without the loser being destroyed and the winner devastated by guilt. In his love life, this recognition meant that both parties might enjoy or be frustrated by each other without the loss of either individual identity or mutual commitment.

As a result of his change, Hank was able to advance his desired role-relationship model and disengage it from the wish–fear dilemma. He was able to form supraordinate configurations and avoid the extreme and antithetical views in his earlier conflicted configuration of role-relationship models. He gained a more flexible understanding of himself and others. Reduction in his unconscious and habitual defensive control processes contributed to this flexibility and sagacity. He became a more friendly, resilient, wise, and reliable person.

Once again, the conflicted role-relationship model configuration

(Figure 8.5) can be contrasted with a more harmonious version (Figure 8.6) that emerged from reschematization processes during the hard work that Hank underwent in psychotherapy. Hank broke free of his rigid wish–fear dilemma: He could compete and win without guilt and he could compete and lose with *vexation* rather than *searing remorse* states. When he lost, he still felt strong in his identity and had respect for the apparently superior rival. He no longer irrationally expected retaliation to harm him when he competed with rivals.

As shown in Figure 8.6, the dreaded state was now a tolerable *vexation*, and he could balance that by frequent achievements of success through cooperation. He could savor occasional states of *victorious joy* from his triumphs in competitions. The overall themes in his life remained, but balance was gained. He still had problematic states in which he competed perhaps longer and harder than was good for his health. In that state he would feel *fatigue and tension*. However, he became capable of early recognition of the realistic power of his rivals. Instead of fighting on to a shameful defeat, he could offer cooperation or even give up a battle while feeling an accepting *calm* within himself (compare the quasi-adaptive compromise in Figure 8.6 with Figure 8.5). His perfectionism over always winning was considerably softened as a result of his work in treatment.

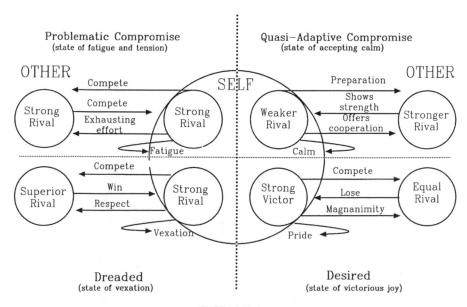

FIGURE 8.6
A MORE HARMONIOUS RRM CONFIGURATION FOR HANK

Both Shirley and Hank balanced identity and relationship. They had fewer undermodulated states of mind and fewer unintended entries into overmodulated states. Shimmering states were less frequent. In social conflicts, they still had periods of negative, distressing moods, but these were tolerable and transient; they knew they could live through them. They did not enter these moods unnecessarily through neurotic repetitions. When these moods did occur, Shirley and Hank were less fearful and would take the risk to live well. They reschematized their systems of beliefs; the process led from a conflicted to a more harmonious constellation of intentions and expectations.

SUMMARY

Integration of character occurs as defensive avoidances are reduced and previously disparate schemas of identity and relationships are reschematized and connected. Emotional experiences are more readily tolerated without explosive shifts in state. Overmodulated states of mind occur less frequently as the danger of undermodulated states is reduced.

Compromise role relationship models remain for use to prevent danger when necessary, but do not need to be constantly used. Character rigidity is reduced, permitting franker engagements with others and a more creative use of personal skills. Integration of character can now occur, which is a high-level combination and connection of previously discordant life themes.

Values that contradicted each other earlier in life are resolved into a set of personal priorities. As a consequence, behavior becomes more predictable. The person will act more responsibly now and in the future.

Conflicts continue in a person with a well-developed character. Integration is an ideal rather than a perfectly achieved goal. No one can work, rest, create, serve others, and amass resources without some discord. Nonetheless, these conflicts are resolved by conscious choices and are not acted out unconsciously, although unconscious processes continue to add passion and creativity.

With character growth, the person gains a sense of strong commitment and a continuity and coherence in identity. Conflicted configurations of how the self relates to others become more harmonious. The journey takes an entire lifetime.

Apter, M. (1989). *Reversal theory: Motivation, emotion, and personality.* New York: Routledge.

Aristotle. (1985). *Nichomachean ethics* (T. Irwin, Trans.). Indianapolis: Hackett.

Arlow, J. A. (1969). Unconscious fantasy and disturbances of conscious experience. *Psychoanalytic Quarterly 38,* 28–51.

Aron, (1996). A meeting of the minds: mutuality in psychoanalysis. NY: Analytic Press.

Assagioli, R. (1965). *Psychosynthesis: A manual of principles and techniques.* New York: Hobb.

Avants, S. K., Margolin, A., & Singer, J. L. (1993). Psychological interventions and research in the oncology setting: An integrative framework. *Psychotherapy 30*(1), 1–10.

Azim, H. F., Piper, W. E., Segal, P. M., & Nixon, G. W. (1991). The Quality of Object Relations Scale. *Bulletin of the Menninger Clinic 55* (3), 323–343.

Baars, B. J. (1986). The cognitive revolution in psychology. N.Y.: Guilford.

Baddeley, A. (1990). *Human memory.* Boston: Allyn and Bacon.

Barrs, B. J. (1992). Divided consciousness or divided self? *Consciousness & Cognition: An International Journal* 1(1), 59–60.

Bartlett, F. C. (1932). *Remembering: A study in experimental and social psychology.* Cambridge: Cambridge University Press.

Baudry, F. (1984). Character: A concept in search of an identity. *Journal of the American Psychiatric Association 32,* 455–477.

Beck, A. T. (1976). *Cognitive therapy and emotional disorders.* New York: International Universities Press.

Beitman, B. D., Goldfried, M. D., Norcross, J. (1989). The movement toward integrating the psychotherapies: An overview. *American Journal of Psychiatry 146* (2), 138–147.

Benjamin, L. S. (1991). Brief SASB-directed reconstructive learning therapy. In P. Crits-Christoph & J. P. Barber (Eds.) *Handbook of short-term dynamic psychotherapy.* New York: Basic Books.

Berne, E. (1961). *Transactional analysis in psychotherapy.* New York: Grove.

Bettleheim, B. (1976). *The uses of enchantment: The meaning and importance of fairy tales.* New York: Knopf.

Bixler, E. O., Kales A., & Soldatos, C. R. (1979). Sleep disorders encountered in medical practice: A national survey of physicians. *Behavioral Medicine 6,* 1–6.

Blatt, J. (1991). Dance/movement therapy: Inherent value of the creative process in psychotherapy. In G. D. Wilson (Ed.), *Psychology and performing arts*, (pp. 283–288). Amsterdam, Netherlands: Swets & Zeitlinger.

Blatt, S. (1990). Interpersonal relatedness and self-definition: Two personality configurations and their implications for psychopathology and psychotherapy. In J. Singer (Ed.), *Repression and dissociation: Implications for personality theory, psychopathology, and health* (pp. 229–236). Chicago: University of Chicago Press.

Blatt, S. J. & Lerner, H. (1983). The psychological assessment of object representations. *Journal of Personality Assessment 47*(2), 7–28.

Blos, P. (1979). *The adolescent passage: Development issues*. New York: International Universities Press.

Bollas, C. (1979). Character: The language of the self. *International Journal of Psychoanalytic Psychotherapy 3*, 397–418.

———. (1987). *The shadow of the object: Psychoanalysis of the unthought known*. New York: Columbia University Press.

Bond, M., Gardner, S., Christian, J. and Sigal, S. J. (1983). Empirical study of self-rated defense styles. *Archives of General Psychiatry 40*, 333–338.

Bonnano, G. A., Keltner, D., Holen, A., and Horowitz, M. J. (1995). When avoiding unpleasant emotions might not be such a bad thing. *Journal of Personality and Social Psychology 69*, 975–990.

Bower, G. H. (1981). Mood and memory. *American Psychologist 36*(2), 129–148.

Bower, G. H., & Gilligan, S. G. (1979). Remembering information related to one's self. *Journal of Research in Personality 13*(4), 420–461.

Bowlby, J. (1969). Attachment. In *Attachment and loss*, Vol. 1, New York: Basic Books.

———. (1973). Separation, anxiety and mourning. In *Attachment and loss*, Vol 2. New York: Basic Books.

Brenner, C. (1982). *The mind in conflict*. New York: International Universities Press.

Bretherton, I. (1985). Attachment theory: Retrospect and prospect. *Monographs of the Society for Research in Child Development 1–2*, 3–35.

Bretherton, I., & Waters, E. (Eds.) (1985). Growing points in attachment theory and research. *Monographs of the Society for Research in Child Development. 50*, 1–320.

Breuer, J., & Freud, S. (1895, 1955). Studies on hysteria. In J. Strachey (Ed.), *The standard edition of the complete psychological works of Sigmund Freud*, Vol 2. London: Hogarth Press.

Brody, S. (1992). *The evolution of character*. New York: International Universities Press.

Bruner, J. S. (1964). The course of cognitive growth. *American Psychologist 19*, 1–20.

Bruner, J. S. (1966). The Processes of Cognitive Growth. Worchester, Mass.: Clark University Press.

Bucci, W. (1985). Dual coding: A cognitive model for psychoanalytic research. *Journal of the American Psychoanalytic Association 33*(3), 571–608.

———. (1993). The development of emotional meaning in free association: A multiple code theory. In A. Wilson & J. E. Gedo (Eds.), *Hierarchical concepts in psychoanalysis: Theory, research, and clinical practice*, New York: Guilford.

———. (1997). *Psychoanalysis and cognitive science: A multiple code theory*. New York: Guilford.

Buie, D. H., & Adler, G. (1982). Definitive treatment of the borderline personality. *International Journal of Psychoanalytic Psychotherapy 9*, 51–87.

Burke, P. J. (1980). The self: Measurement requirements from an interactionist perspective. *Psychoanalytic Quarterly 43*(1), 18–29.

Butler, L. D. & Spiegal, D. (1997). Trauma and memory. In L. J. Dickstein, M. B. Riba, & J. M. Oldham (Eds.), *Review of psychiatry*. Washington, DC: American Psychiatric Press.

Cannon, W. B. (1929). *Bodily changes in pain, hunger, fear and rage*. New York: Appleton.

Carlson, R. (1981). Studies in script theory: I. Adult analogs of a childhood nuclear scene. *Journal of Personality and Social Psychology 4*(3), 533–561.

Carr, V. (1983). The concept of clinical state in psychiatry: A review. *Comprehensive Psychiatry 24*, 370–391.

Carver, C., Scheier, M. F., and Weintraub, J. K. (1989). Assessing coping strategies: A theoretically based approach. *Journal of Personality and Social Psychology 56*, 267–283.

Chalmers, D. J. (1996). *The conscious mind: In search of a fundamental theory*. Oxford: Oxford University Press.

Charcot, J. M. (1877). *Lectures on diseases of the nervous system* (G. Sigerson, Trans.). London: New Sydenham Society.

Churchland, P. S., & Sejnowski, T. J. (1992). *The computational brain*. Boston: MIT Press.

Clark, A. C. (1993). *Associative engines: Connectionism, concepts, and representational change*. Boston: MIT Press.

Cloninger, C. R. (1990). Event-related potentials in populations at genetic risk: Genetic principles and research strategies. In J. W. Rohrbaugh, R. Parasuraman and R. Johnson (Eds.), *Event-related brain potentials: Basic issues and applications*, eds. (pp. 333–342). New York: Oxford University Press.

Cloninger, C. R., Svrakic, D. M., & Przybeck, T. R. (1993). A psychobiological model of temperament and character. *Archives of General Psychiatry 50*(12), 975–990.

Colarusso, C. A., & Nemiroff, R. A. (1981). *Adult development*. New York: Plenum.

Colby, A., Jessor, R., & Shweder, R. (1996). *Essays on ethnography and human development*. Chicago: University of Chicago Press.

Conte, H., & Plutchik, R. (1995). *Ego defenses: Theory and measurement*. New York: Wiley.

Cooper, A. M. (1989). Narcissism and masochishm: The narcissistic-masochistic character. *The Psychiatric Clinics of North America, 12* (3), 541–552.

Cooper, S. (1992). The empirical study of defensive processes: A review. In J. W. Barron, M. N. Eagle, & D. L. Wolitsky (Eds.), *Interface of psychoanalysis and psychology*, Washington, DC: American Psychological Association.

Cramer, P. (1991). *The development of defense mechanisms: Theory, research, and assessment*. New York: Springer-Verlag.

Csikszentmihalyi, M. (1988). The flow experience and its significance for human psychology. In M. Csikszentmihalyi and I. Csikszentmihalyi (Eds.), *Optimal experience: Psychological studies of flow in consciousness* (pp. 15–35). New York: Cambridge University Press.

Dahl, H. (1979). A new psychoanalytic model of motivation. *Psychoanalysis and Contemporary Thought 1*, 373–408.

Damon, W. (1988). Socialization and individuation. In G. Handel (Ed.), *Childhood socialization* (pp. 3–10). New York: Hawthorne.

Damon, W., & Hart, D. (1988). *Self-understanding in childhood and adolescence*. New York: Cambridge University Press.

D'Andrade R. (1991). The identification of schemas in naturalistic data. In M. J. Horowitz (Ed.), *Person schemas and maladaptive interpersonal patterns* (pp. 279–302). Chicago: University of Chicago Press.

Dawkins, R. (1976). *The selfish gene.* Oxford: Oxford University Press.

Dennett, D. (1991). *Consciousness explained.* New York: Little Brown.

Derryberry, D., & Rothbart, M. K. (1988). Arousal, affect, and attention as components of temperament. *Journal of Personality and Social Psychology. 55*(6), 958–966.

Descartes, R. ([1627] 1989). M. Wilson (Ed.), *The Essential Descartes* New York: Mentor Books.

Dixon, N. F. (1981). *Preconscious processing.* New York: Wiley.

Doherty, J., Van Kammen, D. P., Siris, S. G., & Marder, S. R. (1978). Stages of onset of schizophrenic psychosis. *American Journal of Psychiatry 135,* 420–426.

Eells, T., Horowitz, M. J., Singer, J., Salovey, P., Daigle, D., & Turvey, C. (1995). The role relationship models method: A comparison of independently derived case formulations. *Psychotherapy Research 5,* 161–175.

Ekman, P., & Davidson, R. J. (1994). *The nature of emotion.* New York: Oxford University Press.

Eliot, G. (1994). *Impressions of the Theophrastus Such.* London: William Pickering.

Ellenberger, H. F. (1968). The concept of creative illness. *Psychoanalytic Review 55* (3), 442–456.

———. (1970). *Discovery of the unconscious: The history and evolution of dynamic psychiatry.* New York: Basic Books.

Emde, R. N. (1981). Changing models of infancy and the nature of early development. *Journal of the American Psychoanalytic Association 29,* 179–219.

———. (1983). The prerepresentational self and its affective core. *Psychoanalytic Study of the Child 38,* 165–192.

———. (1988). Development terminable and interminable. *International Journal of Psychoanalysis 69,* 23–42.

Erdelyi, M. H. (1984). *Psychoanalysis: Freud's cognitive psychology.* New York: Freeman.

———. (1996). *The recovery of unconscious memories: hypermnesia and reminiscence.* Chicago: University of Chicago Press.

Erikson, E. H. (1950). *Childhood and society.* New York: Norton.

———. (1954). The dream specimen of psychoanalysis. *Journal of the American Psychoanalytic Association 2,* 5–56.

———. (1958). The problem of ego identity. *Journal of the American Psychoanalytic Association 4,* 56–121.

———. (1959). Identity and the life cycle. In E. Erickson (Ed.), *Psychological issues* (pp. 1–167). New York: International Universities Press.

———. (1970). Autobiographic notes on the identity crisis. *Daedalus* 99(4), 730–759.

———. (1982). *The life cycle completed: A review.* New York: Norton.

Fairbairn, W. R. (1952). *Psychoanalytic studies of the personality.* London: Routledge and Kegan Paul.

———. (1954). *An object relations theory of the personality.* New York: Basic Books.

Farthing, G. W. (1992). *The psychology of consciousness.* Englewood Cliffs, NJ: Prentice Hall.

Federn, P. (1952). *Ego psychology and the psychoses.* New York: Basic Books.

Fenichel, O. (1945). *The psychoanalytic theory of neurosis.* New York: Norton.

Ferenczi, S. (1950). *Further contributions to the therapy and techniques of psychoanalysis.* London: Hogarth.

Festinger, L. (1957). *A theory of cognitive dissonance.* New York: Row and Peterson.

Fischer, K. W. & Ayoub, C. (1994). Affective splitting and dissociation in normal and maltreated children: Developmental pathways for self in relationships. In D. Cicchetti & S. Toth (Eds.), *Rochester Symposium on Developmental Psychopathology: The Self and Its Disorders.* Rochester, NY: University of Rochester Press.

Fiske, D. W. (1982). Convergent-discriminant validation in measurements and research strategies. *New Directions for Methodology of Social & Behavioral Science (12),* 77–92.

Fodor, J. A. (1981). The search: Body, mind, and human purpose. *Scientific American 244,* 114–123.

———. (1983). *The modularity of mind: An essay on faculty psychology.* Cambridge, MA: Bradford/MIT Press.

Franz, C. E., & White, K. M. (1985). Individuation and attachment in personality development: Extending Erikson's theory. *Journal of Personality 53(2),* 224–56.

Freud, A. (1936). *The ego and mechanisms of defense.* New York: International Universities Press.

Freud, S. (1900). The interpretation of dreams. In J. Strachey (Ed.), *Standard Edition of the complete psychological works of Sigmund*

Freud (hereafter the Standard Edition), Vol. 4, 5, pp. 1–630. London: Hogarth.

———. (1901). On psychoanalysis. In *Standard edition*, Vol. 12 (pp. 205–212). London: Hogarth.

———. (1905). Three essays on the theory of sexuality. In *Standard edition*, Vol. 7 (pp. 125–248). London: Hogarth.

———. (1908). Characters and anal erotism. In *Standard edition*, Vol. 9 (pp. 167–176). London: Hogarth.

———. (1912a). The dynamics of transference. In *Standard edition*, Vol. 12 (pp. 97–108). London: Hogarth.

———. (1912b). Totem and taboo. In *Standard edition*, Vol. 13 (pp. 1–164). London: Hogarth.

———. (1914a). On narcissism: An introduction. In *Standard edition*, Vol. 14 (pp. 67–104). London: Hogarth.

———. (1914b). Remembering, repeating and working through. In *Standard edition*, Vol. 12 (pp. 145–156). London: Hogarth.

———. (1915). The unconscious. In *Standard edition*, Vol. 14, (pp. 159–218). London: Hogarth.

———. (1920a). *A general introduction to psychoanalysis*. New York: Boni and Liveright.

———. (1920b). Beyond the pleasure principle. In *Standard edition*, Vol. 18 (pp. 3–66). London: Hogarth.

———. (1923). The ego and id. In *Standard edition*, Vol. 19 (pp. 1–66). London: Hogarth.

———. (1926). Inhibition, symptoms, and anxiety. In *Standard edition*, Vol. 19 (pp. 87–156). London: Hogarth.

———. (1927). Humour. In *Standard edition*, Vol. 21 (pp. 160–166). London: Hogarth.

Freud, S. & J. Breuer. ([1893–1895] 1955). Studies on hysteria. In J. Strachey (Ed.), *Standard edition*, vol. 2 (pp. 1–320). London: Hogarth.

Furster, J. M. (1991): *The prefrontal cortex: Anatomy, physiology, and neuropsychology of the frontal lobe*, 2d ed. New York: Raven.

Gaarter, K. (1971). Control of states of consciousness: Attainment through external feedback augmenting control of psychophysiological variables. *Archives of General Psychiatry 25*, 436–441.

Gardner, H. (1985). *Frames of mind: The theory of multiple intelligences*. New York: Basic Books.

Gedo, J., & Goldberg, A. (1973). *Models of the mind*. Chicago: University of Chicago Press.

George, C., & Main, M. (1979). Social interactions of young and abused children: Approach, avoidance, and aggression. *Child Development 50*, 306–318.

Gill, M., & Holzman, P. (1976). Psychology versus metapsychology. *Psychological Issues 9, Monograph 36*. New York: International Universities Press.

Goldberg, A. (1994). Farewell to the object analyst. *International Journal of Psychoanalysis 75*, 21–30.

Goldfried, M. R. (1996). Toward a common language for case formulation. *Journal of Psychotherapeutic Integration 5*, 221–244.

Goldsmith, H. H., & Campos, J. J. (1982). Toward a theory of infant temperament. In R. N. Emde and R. J. Harmon (Eds.). *The development of attachment and affiliative systems*, New York: Plenum.

Goleman, D. (1995). *Emotional intelligence*. New York: Bantam Books.

Goodman, A. (1991). Organic unity theory: The mind–body problem revisited. *American Journal of Psychiatry 148*(5), 553–563.

Graf, P. & Masson, M. E. J. (Eds.). (1993) *Implicit memory: New directions in cognition, development, and neuropsychology*. New York: Academic Press.

Gray, P. (1982). "Developmental lag" in the evolution of analytic technique. *Journal of the American Psychoanalytic Association 30*, 621–639.

———. (1994). *The ego and analysis of defense*. Northvale, NJ: Aronson.

Greenacre, P. (1958). Early psychical determinants in the development of the sense of identity. *Journal of the American Psychoanalytic Association 6*, 131–142, 612–627.

Greenberg, J. & Mitchell, S. (1983). *Object relations in psychoanalytic theory*. Boston: Harvard University Press.

Greenson, R. R. (1967). *The technique and practice of psychoanalysis*. New York: International Universities Press.

Greenspan, S. I. (1994). *Developmentally based psychotherapy*. Madison: International University Press.

Greenspan, S. I., & Lourie, R. S. (1981). Developmental structuralist approach to the classification of adaptive and pathological personality organizations: Infancy and early childhood. *American Journal of Psychiatry 136*, 725–735.

Guntrip, H. (1961). *Personality structure and human interaction*. New York: International Universities Press.

———. (1971). *Psychoanalytic theory, therapy, and the self*. New York: Basic Books.

Gustafson, J. (1986). *The complex secret of brief therapy.* New York: Norton.

Haan, N. (1977). *Coping and defending: Processes of self-environment organization.* New York: Academic Press.

Hart, D., Stinson, C., Field, N., Ewert, M., & Horowitz, M. (1995). A semantic space approach to representations of self and other in pathological grief: A case study. *Psychological Science 6*(2), 96–100.

Hartmann, H. (1964). *Essays on ego psychology: Selected problems in psychoanalytic theory.* New York: International Universities Press.

Havens, L. (1987). *Approaches to the mind.* Cambridge, MA: Harvard University Press.

Hebb, D. O. (1968). Concerning imagery. *Psychological Review 75*(6), 466–477.

Hentschel, U., Smith, G., Ehlers, W., & Draguns, J. G. (Eds). (1993). *The concept of defense mechanisms in contemporary psychology.* New York: Springer-Verlag.

Higgins, E. T. (1987). Self-discrepancy: A theory relating self and affect. *Psychological Review 94*(3), 319–340.

Hobson, R. P. (1994). On developing a mind. *British Journal of Psychiatry 165*(5), 577–581.

Horowitz, F. D. (1987). *Exploring developmental theories: Toward a structural behavioral model of development.* Hillsdale, NJ: Erlbaum.

Horowitz, M. J. (1966). Body image. *Archives of General Psychiatry 14,* 456–460.

———. (1967). Visual imagery and cognitive organization. *American Journal of Psychiatry 123,* 938–946.

———. (1969). Psychic trauma: Return of images after a stress film. *Archives of General Psychiatry 20,* 552–559.

———. (1969). Flashbacks: Recurrent intrusive images after the use of LSD. *American Journal of Psychiatry 126,* 565–569.

———. (1970). *Image formation and cognition.* New York: Appleton Century Crofts.

———. (1972a). Image formation: Clinical observations and cognitive model. In P. Sheehon (Ed.), *The Nature and Function of Imagery.* New York: Academic Press.

———. (1972b). Modes of representation of thought. *Journal of the American Psychoanalytic Association 20,* 793–819.

———. (1973). Phase-oriented treatment of stress response syndromes. *American Journal of Psychotherapy 27*(4), 506–515.

————. (1974). Stress response syndromes: Character style and brief psychotherapy. *Archives of General Psychiatry 31*, 768–781.

————. (1975a). A cognitive model of hallucinations. *American Journal of Psychiatry 132*, 789–795.

————. (1975b). Intrusive and repetitive thoughts after experimental stress: A summary. *Archives of General Psychiatry 32*, 1457–1463.

————. (1977a). Cognitive and interactive aspects of splitting. *American Journal of Psychiatry 134*: 549–553.

————. (1977b). *Stress response syndromes*, 3d ed. New York: Aronson.

————. (1979a). Depressive disorders in response to loss. In I. G. Sarason & C. D. Spielberger (Eds.), *Stress and Anxiety* (pp. 235–255). New York: Hemisphere Publishing Co.

————. (1979b). *States of mind: Configurational analysis of individual personality*. New York: Plenum.

————. (1981). Self-righteous rage and the attribution of blame. *Archives of General Psychiatry 38*, 1233–1238.

————. (1983a). *Image formation and psychotherapy*. Northvale, NJ: Aronson.

————. (1983b). Stress response syndromes and their treatment. In L. Goldberger & S. Bresnitz (Eds.), *Handbook of Stress* (pp. 711–732). New York: Free Press.

————. (1984). Stress response syndromes and the mechanisms of defense. In H. Goldman (Ed.), *Review of Psychiatry* (pp. 42–50). Palo Alto, CA: Lange.

————. (1987). *States of mind: Configurational analysis of individual personality*, 2nd ed. New York: Plenum.

————. (1988a). *Introduction to psychodynamics: A new synthesis*. New York: Basic Books.

————. (1988b). Formulation of states of mind in psychotherapy. *American Journal of Psychotherapy 42*(4), pp. 77–90.

————. (1988c). Psychodynamic phenomena and their explanation. In M. Horowitz (Ed.), *Psychodynamics and cognition* (pp. 3–20), Chicago: University of Chicago Press.

————. (1989a). Clinical phenomenology of the narcissistic pathology. *Psychiatric Clinics of North America 12*, 531–539.

————. (1989b). Relationship schema formulation: Role-relationship models and intrapsychic conflict. *Psychiatry 52*(3), 260–274.

————. (1989c). *Nuances of technique in dynamic psychotherapy*. Northvale, NJ: Aronson.

————. (1990). A model of mourning: Change in schemas of self and other. *Journal of the American Psychoanalytic Association 38*(2), 297–324.

————. (1991a). (Ed.) *Person schemas and maladaptive interpersonal patterns.* Chicago: University of Chicago Press.

————. (1991b). States, schemas, and control: General theories for psychotherapy integration. *Journal of Psychotherapy Integration 2* (2), 85–102.

————. (1992). Formulation of states of mind in psychotherapy. In N. G. Hamilton (Ed.), *From inner resources: New directions in object relations psychotherapy* (pp. 75–83). Northvale, NJ: Aronson.

————. (1993). Defensive control of states and person schemas. *Journal of the American Psychoanalytic Association 41*, 67–89.

————. (1994). Configurational analysis and the use of role-relationship models to understand transference. *Psychotherapy Research 3*, 184–196.

————. (1997a). Configurational analysis for case formulation. *Psychiatry 60*, 111–119.

————. (1997b). *Formulation as a basis for planning psychotherapy.* Washington, DC: Amer. Psychiatric Press.

————. (1997c). Organizational levels of self and other schematization. In P. M. Westenberg, R. G. Rogers, L. D. Cohn, & A. Blasi (Eds.), *Personality development.* New York: Erlbaum.

————. (1997). *Stress response syndromes*, 3rd ed. Northvale, NJ: Aronson.

————. (1997d). Psychotherapy of the histrionic personality disorder. *Journal of Psychotherapy Practice and Research 6*, 93–107.

Horowitz, M. J., Adams, J., & Rutkin, B. (1967). Dream scintillations. *Psychosomatic Medicine 29*, 284–292.

Horowtiz, M. J., & Arthur, R. (1988). Narcissistic rage in leaders: The intersection of individual dynamics and group process. *International Journal of Social Psychiatry 34*, 135–141.

Horowitz, M. J., & Becker, S. S. (1971a). Cognitive response to stress and experimental demand. *Journal of Abnormal Psychology 78*, 86–92.

————. (1971b). Cognitive response to stressful stimuli. *Archives of General Psychiatry 25*, 419–428.

————. (1972). Cognitive response to stress: Experimental studies of a "compulsion to treat trauma." In R. Holt & E. Peterfreund (Eds.),

Psychoanalysis and contemporary science, Vol. 1 (pp. 258–305). New York: Macmillan.

———. (1973). Cognitive response to erotic and stressful films. *Archives of General Psychiatry 29*, 81–84.

Horowitz, M. J., Becker, S. S., & Malone, P. (1973). Stress: Different effects in patients and non-patients. *Journal of Abnormal Psychology 82*, 547–551.

Horowitz, M. J., Bonanno, G. A., & Holen, A. (1993). Pathological grief: Diagnosis and explanation. *Psychosomatic Medicine 55*, 260–273.

Horowitz, M. J., Cooper, S., Fridhandler, B., Perry, J. C., Bond, M., & Vaillant, G. (1992). Control processes and defense mechanisms. *Journal of Psychotherapy Practice and Research 1*(4), 324–336.

Horowitz, M. J. & Eells, T. (1993a). Case formulations using role-relationship model configurations: A reliability study. *Psychotherapy Research 3*(1), 57–68.

———. (1993b). Role-relationship model configurations: A method of psychotherapy case formulation. *Psychotherapy Research 3*, 57–68.

Horowitz, M. J., Eells, T., Singer, J., & Salovey, P. (1995). Role relationship models for case formulation. *Archives of General Psychiatry 52*(8), 625–632, 654–656.

Horowitz, M. J., Ewert, M., & Milbrath, C. M. (1996). States of emotional control during psychotherapy. *Journal of Psychotherapy Research and Practice 5*, 20–25.

Horowitz, M. J., Fridhandler, B., & Stinson, C. (1991). Person schemas and emotion. *Journal of the American Psychoanalytic Association 39*, 173–208.

Horowitz, M. J., Hulley, S., Alvarez, W., Billings, J., Benfari, R., Blair, S., Borhani, N., & Simon, N. (1980). News of risk for early heart disease as a stressful event. *Psychosomatic Medicine 42*, 37–46.

Horowitz, M., Kernberg, O., & Weinschel, W. (Eds.). (1993). *Psychic structure and psychic change*. New York: International University Press.

Horowitz, M. J., Markman, H. C., Stinson, C. H., Ghannam, J. H. & Fridhandler, B. (1990). A classification theory of defense. In J. Singer (Ed.), *Repression and dissociation: Implications for personality theory, psychopathology and health* (pp. 61–84). Chicago: University of Chicago Press.

Horowitz, M. J., Marmar, C., Krupnik, J., Wilner, N., Kaltreider, N., & Rosenbaum, R. (1984). *Personality styles and brief psychotherapy.* New York: Basic Books.

Horowitz, M. J., Marmar, C., Weiss, D. S., DeWitt, K., & Rosenbaum, R. (1984). Brief psychotherapy of bereavement reactions: the relationship of process to outcome. *Archives of General Psychiatry 41,* 438–448.

Horowitz, M. J., Marmar, C., Weiss, D., Kaltreider, N., & Wilner, N. (1986). Comprehensive analysis of change after brief dynamic psychotherapy. *American Journal of Psychiatry 143*(5), 582–589.

Horowitz, M. J., Marmar, C., & Wilner, N. (1979). Analysis of patient states and state transitions. *Journal of Nervous and Mental Disease 167,* 91–99.

Horowitz, M. J., Milbrath, C., Bonanno, G., Stinson, C., Field, N. & A., H. (In Press). Predictors of complicated grief. *Journal of Personal and Interpersonal Loss.*

Horowitz, M. J., Milbrath, C., Ewert, M. Sonneborn, D., & Stinson, C. H. (1994). Cyclical patterns of states of mind in psychotherapy. *American Journal of Psychiatry. 151*(12), 1767–1770.

Horowitz, M. J., Milbrath, C., Jordon, D. S., Stinson, C. H., Ewert, M., Redington, D. J., Fridhandler, B., Reidbord, S. P., & Hartley, D. (1994). Expressive and defensive behavior during discourse on unresolved topics: A single case study. *Journal of Personality 62*(4), 527–563.

Horowitz, M. J., Milbrath, C., Reidbord, S., & Stinson, C. H. (1993). Elaboration and dyselaboration: Measures of expression and defense in discourse. *Psychotherapy Research 3*(4), 278–293.

Horowitz, M. J., Milbrath, C., & Stinson, C. (1995). Signs of defensive control locate conflicted topics in discourse. *Archives of General Psychiatry 52*(12), 1040–1057.

Horowitz, M. J., Sonneborn, D., Sugahara, C., & Maercker, A. (1996). Self Regard: A new measure. *American Journal of Psychiatry 153*(3), 382–385.

Horowitz, M. J., Stinson, C. H., & Milbrath, C. (1996). Role relationship models: A person schematic method for inferring beliefs about identity and social action. In A. Colby, R. Jessor, & R. Shweder (Eds.), *Essays on Ethnography and Human Development* (pp. 253–274). Chicago: University of Chicago Press.

Horowitz, M. J., & Stinson, C. H. (1994). Defenses as aspects of person schemas and control processes. In H. Conte & R. Plutchik

(Eds), *Ego defenses: Theory and measurement* (pp. 79–97). NY: Wiley.

———. (1995). Consciousness and processes of control. *Journal of Psychotherapy Practice and Research 4*(2), 123–139.

Horowitz, M. J., Stinson, C., Curtis, D., Ewert, M., Redington, D., Singer, J., Bucci, W., Mergenthaler, E., & Milbrath, C. (1993). Topics and signs: Defensive control of emotional expression. *Journal of Consulting and Clinical Psychology 61*(3), 421–430.

Horowitz, M. J., & Wilner, N. (1976). Stress films, emotion, and cognitive response. *Archives of General Psychiatry 30*, 1339–1344.

Horowitz, M. J., Wilner, N., & Alvarez, W. (1979). The impact of event scale: A measure of subjective stress. *Psychomatic Medicine 41* (3), 209–218.

Horowitz, M. J., Wilner, N., Kaltreider, N., & Alvarez, W. (1980). Signs and symptoms of post-traumatic stress disorder. *Archives of General Psychiatry 37*, 85–92.

Horowitz, M. J., Wilner, N., Marmar, C., & Krupnik, J. (1980). Pathological grief and the activation of latent self images. *American Journal of Psychiatry 137*, 1157–1162.

Horowitz, M. J., & Zilberg, N. (1983). Regressive alterations in the self-concept. *American Journal of Psychiatry 140*(3), 284–289.

Horowitz, M. J., Znoj, H., & Stinson, C. (1996). Defensive control processes: Use of theory in research, formulation, and therapy of stress response syndromes. In M. Zeidner & N. Endler (Eds.), *Handbook of Coping*, (pp. 532–553). New York: Wiley.

Hunt, H. T. (1995). *On the nature of consciousness: Cognitive, phenomenological, and transpersonal perspectives.* New Haven, CT: Yale University Press.

Jackendoff, R. (1987). *Consciousness and the computational mind.* Boston: MIT Press.

Jacobson, E. (1964). *The self in the object world.* New York: International Universities Press.

James, W. ([1890] 1950). *The principles of psychology.* New York: Dover.

———. (1910). *Psychology: The briefer course.* New York: Holt.

Janet, P. (1925). *Psychological healing: A historical and clinical study,* Vols. 1 and 2 (E. Paul, Trans.). London: Allen and Unwin.

———. (1965). *The major symptoms of hysteria.* New York: Hafner.

Janis, I. (1969). *Stress and frustration.* New York: Harcourt Brace Jovanovich.

Johnson, S. M. (1994) *Character styles.* New York: Norton.

Johnson-Laird, P. N. (1988a). A taxonomy of thinking. In R. J. Sternberg and E. E. Smith (Eds.), *The psychology of human thought* (pp. 429–457) New York: Cambridge University Press.

———. (1988b). *The computer and the mind: An introduction to cognitive science.* Boston: Harvard University Press.

Jones, E. (1929). Fear, guilt and hate. *International Journal of Psycho-Analysis* 10, 383–397.

Jung, C. G. (1933). *Modern man in search of a soul.* New York: Harcourt.

———. (1939). *The integration of personality.* New York: Farrar and Rinehart.

———. (1959). *The archetypes and the collective unconscious.* New York: Pantheon.

Kagan, R. (1982). *The developing self.* Cambridge, MA: Harvard University Press.

Kalthoff, R., & Neimeyer, R. (1993). Self complexity and psychological distress: A test of the buffering model. *International Journal of Personal Construct Psychology* 6(4): 327–349.

Kant, I. ([1781] 1969). *Critique of pure reason.* New York: St. Martin's.

Katz, A. N. (1987). Self-reference in the encoding of creative-relevant traits. *Journal of Personality* 55(1), 97–120.

Kelly, G. A. (1955). *The psychology of personal constructs,* Vols. 1 and 2. New York: Norton.

Kernberg, O. F. (1967). Borderline personality organization. *Journal of the American Psychoanalytic Association* 15, 41–68.

———. (1969). A contribution to the ego-psychological critique of the Kleinian school. *International Journal of Psycho-Analysis* 50(3): 317–333.

———. (1976). *Object relations theory and clinical psychoanalysis.* New York: Aronson.

———. (1982). Self, ego, affects, and drives. *Journal of the American Psychoanalytic Association* 30(4): 893–917.

———. (1984). *Object-relations theory and clinical psychoanalysis.* New York: Aronson.

———. (1992). *Aggression in personality disorders and perversions.* New Haven, CT: Yale University Press.

Kets de Vries, M. F. R., & Perzow, S., (Eds.) (1991). *Handbook of character studies: Psychoanalytic explorations.* Madison, CT: International Universities Press.

Kihlstrom, J. F. (1987). The cognitive unconscious. *Science 237*, 1445–1452.

———. (1993). Consciousness and me-ness. In J. Cohen and J. Schooler (Eds.), *Scientific approaches to the question of consciousness*. Hillsdale, NJ: Erlbaum.

Kihlstrom, J., & Cantor, N. (1994). Mental representations of the self. In L. Berkowitz (Ed.), *Advances in experimental social psychology*, (pp. 1–47). New York: Academic Press.

Klaif, C. H. (1984). Emerging concepts of the self: A Jungian view. *Journal of Analytical Psychology 30*, 41–55.

Klein, G. S. (1976). *Psychoanalytic theory: An exploration of essentials*. New York: International Universities Press.

Klein, M. (1948). *Mourning and its relation to manic depressive states: Contributions to psychoanalysis*. London: Hogarth.

Kluft, E. S. (Ed.) (1992). *Expressive and functional therapies in the treatment of multiple personality disorder*. Springfield, IL: C. C. Thomas.

Kluft, R. P. (Ed.) (1989). *Treatment of victims of sexual abuse*. Philadelphia: Saunders.

Knapp, P. H. (1991). Self–other schemas: Core organizers of human experience. In M. J. Horowitz (Ed.), *Person schemas and maladaptive interpersonal patterns* (pp. 81–104). Chicago: University of Chicago Press.

Kohlberg, L. (1969). Stage and sequence: The cognitive developmental approach to socialization. In D. A. Goslin (Ed.), *Handbook of socialization and research* (pp. 93–120). Chicago: Rand McNally.

Kohler, W. (1929). *Gestalt psychology*. New York: Liveright.

Kohut, H. (1971). *Analysis of the self*. New York: International Universities Press.

———. (1972). Thoughts on narcissism and narcissistic rage. *Psychoanalytic Study of the Child 27*, 360–400.

———. (1977). *Restoration of the self*. New York: International Universities Press.

Kosslyn, S. M. (1981). The medium and the message in mental imagery: A theory. *Psychological Review 88*, 46–66.

———. (1990). Mental imagery. In S. Osherson, S. Kosslyn, & J. Hollervach (Eds.), *Visual Cognition and Action: An Invitation to Cognitive Science*, 2 (pp. 2–40). Cambridge, MA: MIT Press.

———. (1994). *Image and brain: The resolution of the imagery debate*. Cambridge, MA: MIT Press.

Kosslyn, S. M., & Koenig, O. (1992). *Wet mind: The new cognitive neuroscience*. New York: Free Press.

Kovacs, M., & Beck, A. (1978). Maladaptive cognitive structures in depression. *American Journal of Psychiatry 135*(5), 525–533.

Kreitler, H., & Kreitler, S. (1982). The theory of cognitive orientation: Widening the scope of behavioral prediction. In Maher (Ed.), *Experimental personality research* (pp. 65–90). New York: Springer.

Krystal, H. (1994). Self- and object-representation in alcoholism and other drug-dependence: Implications for therapy. In J. D. Levin & R. H. Weiss, (Eds.), *The dynamics and treatment of alcoholism: Essential papers*, (pp. 300–309). Northvale, NJ: Aronson.

Kubie, L. S. (1943). The use of induced hypnotic reveries in the recovery of repressed amnesic data. *Bulletin of the Menninger Clinic 7*, 172–185.

Kuhn, T. S. (1970). *The structure of scientific revolutions*. Chicago: University of Chicago Press.

Landrum, P. E. (1993). Sensitivity of implicit memory to input processing and the Zeigarnik effect. *Journal of General Psychology 120*, 91–98.

Lang, P. J. (1994). The motivational organization of emotion: Affect-reflex connections. In S. H. M. van Goozen, N. E. Van de Poll, & J. A. Sergeant (Eds.), *Emotions: Essays on emotion theory*, (pp. 61–93). Hillsdale, NJ: Erlbaum.

Lazarus, R. S. (1966). *Psychological stress and the coping process*. New York: McGraw-Hill.

———. (1991). *Emotion and adaptation*. New York: Oxford University Press.

Ledoux, J. E. (1995). Emotion: Clues from the brain. *Annual Review of Psychology 46*, 209–235.

Levinson, D. (1978). *The seasons of a man's life*. New York: Ballantine Books.

Lewin, K. (1935). *A dynamic theory of personality*. New York: McGraw-Hill.

Lichtenstein, H. (1977). *The dilemma of human identity*. New York: Aronson.

Linville, P. W. (1982). Affective consequence of complexity regarding the self and others. In M. S. Clark and S. T. Fiske (Eds.), *Affect and cognition: 17th Annual Carnegie Symposium on Cognition* (pp. 193–211). Hillsdale, NJ: Erlbaum.

————. (1985). Self complexity and effective extremity: Don't put all your eggs in one cognitive basket. *Social Cognition 3*, 94–120.

Linville, P., & Carlston, D. (1994). Social cognition of the self. In P. G. Devine, D. Hamilton, & T. Ostrom (Eds), *Social cognition: It's impact on social psychology* (pp. 143–193). New York: Academic Press.

Locke, E. A. (1995). Beyond determinism and materialism, or Isn't it time we took consciousness seriously? *Journal of Behavior Therapy and Experimental Psychiatry 26*(3), 265–273.

Locke, J. ([1690]1894). *An essay concerning human understanding*. (A. C. Fraser, Ed.). Oxford: Clarendon.

Loevinger, J. (1976). *Ego development*. San Francisco: Jossey-Bass.

Loewald, H. (1957). On the therapeutic action of psychoanalysis. (Ed.), *Papers on Psychoanalysis* (pp. 221–256). New Haven, CT: Yale University Press.

Luborsky, L. (1977). Measuring a pervasive psychic structure in psychotherapy: The core conflictual relationship theme. In N. Freedman & S. S. Grand (Eds.), *Communicative structures and psychic structures*. New York: Plenum.

————. (1984). *Principles of psychoanalytic psychotherapy: A manual for supportive expressive treatment*. New York: Basic Books.

Luborsky, L., & Crits-Christoph, P. (1990). *Understanding transference: The CCRT method*. New York: Basic Books.

Mahler, M. (1968). *On human symbiosis and the vicissitudes of individuation*. New York: International Universities Press.

Main, M. (1975). Mother-avoiding babies. Paper presented at biennial meeting of Society for Research in Child Development.

Main, M., & Hesse, E. (1990). Parents' unresolved traumatic experiences are related to infant disorganized attachment status: Is frightened and/or frightening parental behavior the linking mechanism? In M. Greenberg, D. Cichetti, & M. Cummings (Eds.), *Attachment in the preschool years: Theory, research, and intervention* (pp. 161–182). Chicago: University of Chicago Press.

Malan, D. H. (1976). *Toward the validation of dynamic psychotherapy*. New York: Plenum.

Mandler, G. A. (1964). The interruption of behavior. In D. Levine (Ed.), *Nebraska symposium on motivation* (pp. 163–219). Lincoln, NE: University of Nebraska Press.

————. (1975). *Mind and emotion*. New York: Wiley.

———. (1989) Memory: Conscious and unconscious. In P. R. Solomon, G. R. Goethals, C. M. Kelley, & B. R. Stephens (Eds.), *Memory, interdisciplinary approaches* (pp. 84–106). New York: Springer-Verlag.

Markus, H. (1977). Self-schemata and processing information about the self. *Journal of Personality and Social Psychology 35*(2), 63–78.

Markus, H., & Wurf, E. (1987). The dynamic self-concept: A social psychological perspective. *Annual Review of Psychology 38*, 299–337.

Marmar, C., & Horowitz, M. J. (1986). Phenomenological analysis of splitting. *Psychotherapy 23*(1), 21–29.

Maslow, A. H. (1962). *Toward a psychology of being*. Princeton, NJ: Van Nostrand.

Mayman, M. (1968). Early memories and character structure. *Journal of Projective Techniques and Personality Assessment 32*(4), 303–316.

McClelland, J. L., & Rummelhart, D. E. (1988). *Explorations in parallel distributed processing*. Cambridge, MA.: MIT Press.

McFarlane, A. H., Norman, G. R., Streiner, D. L., & Roy, R. G. (1984). Characteristics and correlates of effective and ineffective social supports. *Journal of Psychosomatic Research 28*(6), 501–510.

McKellar, P. (1957). *Imagination and thinking*. New York: Basic Books.

McWilliams, N. (1994). *Psychoanalytic diagnosis: Understanding personality structure in the clinical process*. New York: Guilford.

Menninger, K. (1958). *Theory of psychoanalytic technique*. New York: Basic Books.

Milbrath, C., Bauknight, R., & Horowitz, M. J. (1995). Topic sequences and change in psychotherapy. *Psychotherapy Research 5*, 199–217.

Minsky, M. (1980). *Mentopolis (the society of mind)*. Stuggart: Klett-Cotta.

Modell, A. (1975). A narcissistic defence against affects and the illusion of self-sufficiency. *International Journal of Psychoanalysis 56*, 275–282.

Money, J., & Ehrhardt, A. A. (1972). *Man and woman, boy and girl: The differentiation and démorphism of gender identity from inception to maturity*. Baltimore: Johns Hopkins University Press.

Murray, H. A. (1938). *Explorations in personality*. New York: Oxford University Press.

Neimeyer, R. (1986). *The development of personal construct psychology*. Lincoln, NE: University of Nebraska Press.

Neisser, U. (1988). Five kinds of self knowledge. *Philosophical Psychology 1*, 35–59.

———. (1990). Learning from the children. In R. Fivush & J. Hudson (Eds.), *Knowing and remembering in young children*. New York: Cambridge University Press.

Ogden, T. H. (1992). *The matrix of mind: Object relations and the psychoanalytic dialogue*. Hillsdale, NJ: Aronson.

Oremland, J., & Gill, M. M. (Eds.). (1992). *Interpretation and interaction: Psychoanalysis or psychotherapy*. New York: Analytic Press.

Paivio, A. (1989). A dual coding perspective on imagery and the brain. In J. W. Brown (Ed.), *Neuropsychology and Visual Perception* (pp. 1–267) Hillsdale, NJ: Erlbaum.

Pavlov, I. D. [(1928–1941] 1972). *Lectures on conditional reflexes*. New York: International Universities Press.

Perry, J. C., & Kardos, M. E. (1995). A review of the Defense Mechanism Rating Scales. In H. Conte & R. Plutchik (Eds.), *Ego Defenses: Theory and measurement*, (pp. 283–299) New York: Wiley.

Perry, J. C., Cooper, A. M., & Michels, R. (1987). The psychodynamic formulation. *American Journal of Psychiatry 144*, 543–550.

Peterfreund, E. (1971). Information, systems, and psychoanalysis: An evolutionary biological approach to psychoanalytic theory. *Psychological Issues 7* (1/2). Monograph 25/26.

Piaget, J. (1930). *The child's conception of physical causality*. New York: Harcourt.

Pine, F. (1985). *Development theory and clinical process*. New Haven, CT: Yale University Press.

———. (1990). *Drive, ego, object, self*. New York: Basic Books.

Piper, W. E., Azim, H. F., Joyce, A. S., & McCallum, M. (1991a). Quality of object relations versus interpersonal functioning as predictors of therapeutic alliance and psychotherapy outcome. *Journal of Nervous & Mental Disease 179*(7), 432–438.

———. (1991b). Transference interpretations, therapeutic alliance, and outcome in short-term individual psychotherapy. *Archives of General Psychiatry 48*(10), 946–953.

Pittman, R. K., Orr, S. P., Forque, D. F., et al. (1990) Psychophysiologic responses to combat imagery of Vietnam veterans with post-traumatic stress disorder versus other anxiety disorders. *Journal of Abnormal Psychology 99*, 49–51.

Plomin, R. and Dunn, J., (Eds.) (1986). *The study of temperament: Changes, continuities, and challenges*. Hillsdale, NJ: Erlbaum.

Pope, K. S., & Singer, J. L. (1978). *The stream of consciousness*. New York: Plenum.

Posner, M. I. (Ed.) (1989). *Foundations of cognitive science*. Boston: MIT Press.

————. (1990). Hierarchical distributed networks in the neuropsychology and neurolinguistics. In A. Caramazza (Ed.), *Cognitive Neuropsychology and Neurolinguistics: Advances in Models of Cognitive Function and Impairment* (pp. 187–210). Hillsdale, NJ: Erlbaum

Pylyshyn, Z. (1984). *Computation and cognition*. Cambridge, MA: Bradford/MIT Press.

————. (1994). Mental pictures on the brain. *Nature 372*, 289–290.

Rajaram, S. (1993). Remembering and knowing: Two means of access to the personal past. *Memory and Cognition 21*, 89–102.

Reich, W. (1949). *Character analysis*. New York: Orgone Institute Press.

Renick, O. (1990). Comments on the clinical analysis of anxiety and depressive affect. *Psychoanalysis Quarterly 59*, 226–248.

Richman, N. E., & Sokolove, R. L. (1992). The experience of aloneness, object representation, and evocative memory in borderline and neurotic patients. *Psychoanalytic Psychology 9*(1), 77–91.

Rogers, T. B., Kuiper, N. A., & Kirker, W. S. (1977). Self-reference and the encoding of personal information. *Journal of Personality and Social Psychology 35*(9), 677–688.

Rogers, T. B., Kuiper, N. A., & Rogers, J. P. (1979). Symbolic distance and congruity effects for paired-comparison judgements of degree of self-reference. *Journal of Research in Personality 13*(4), 433–449.

Rowan, J. (1990). *Subpersonalities*. London: Routledge.

Ruesch, J., & Bateson, G. (1968). *Communication: The social matrix of psychiatry*. New York: Norton.

Rumelhart, D. E., McClelland, J. L., & PDP Research Group. (1986). *Parallel distributed processing: Exploration in the microstructure of cognition, Vol. I: Foundations*. Cambridge, MA: MIT Press.

Ryle, A. (1975). *Frames and cages*. New York: International Universities Press.

Sandler, J. (1960). The background of safety. *International Journal of Psychoanalysis 41*, 352–356.

Sandler, J., & Sandler, A. M. (1984). The past unconsciousness, the present unconscious, and interpretation of the transference. *Psychoanalytic Inquiry 4*, 367–400.

Sarnoff, C. (1976). *Latency*. New York: Aronson.

Sass, L. A. (1992). *Madness and modernism: Insanity in the light of modern art, literature, and thought*. New York: Basic Books.

Schacter, D. L. (1987). Implicit memory: History and current status. *Journal of Experimental Psychology: Learning, Memory and Cognition 11*, 501–518.

Schacter, D., & Tulving, E. (Eds.) (1994). *Memory systems*. Cambridge, MA: MIT Press.

Schafer, R. (1992). *Retelling a life: Narration and dialogue in psychoanalysis*. New York: Basic Books.

Schilder, P. (1950). *The image and appearance of the human body*. New York: International Universities Press.

Selye, H. (1976). *Stress in health and disease*. Boston: Butterworth.

Singer, J. L., & Salovey, P. (1993). *The remembered self: Emotion and memory in personality*. New York: Free Press.

Singer, J. L. (1966). *Daydreaming*. New York: Random House.

———. (1985). Transference and the human condition: A cognitive-affective perspective. *Psychoanalytic Psychology 2*, 189–219.

———. (1987). Private experience and public action: The study of on-going conscious thought. In J. Aronoff, A. Rabin, & R. A. Zucker (Eds.), *The emergence of personality* (pp. 105–146). New York: Springer-Verlag.

———. (1990). Beyond repression and the defenses. In J. Singer (Ed.), *Repression and dissociation: Implications for personality theory, psychopathology, and health* Chicago: University of Chicago Press.

Singer, J. L., & Salovey, P. (1991). Organized knowledge structures and personality: Person schemas, self-schemas, prototypes and scripts. In M. J. Horowitz (Ed.), *Person schemas and maladaptive interpersonal patterns* (pp. 33–80). Chicago: University of Chicago Press.

Slap, J. W., & Slap-Shelton, L. (1991). *The schema in clinical psychoanalysis*. Hillsdale, NJ: Analytic Press.

Sperling, M. B., & Berman, W. H. (1994). *Attachment in adults*. New York: Guilford.

Spiegel, D. (1994). *Dissociative experiences*. Washington, DC: American Psychiatric Press.

Spitz, R. A. (1960). *The first year of life*. New York: International Universities Press.

Squire, L. R. (1986). Mechanisms of memory. *Science 232*, 1612–1619.

Squire, L. R., Knowlton, B., & Musen, G. (1993). The structure and organization of memory. *Annual Review of Psychology 44*, 453–495.

Squires, R. (1969). Memory unchained. *Philosophical Review* 78(2), 178–196.

Sroufe, L. A. (1979). The coherence of individual development: Early care attachment, and subsequent developmental issues. *American Psychologist 34*, 834–841.

Sroufe, L. A., & Fleeson, J. (1986). Attachment and the construction of relationships. In W. P. Hartup & Z. Rubin (Eds.), *Relationships and development* (pp. 289–319). Hillsdale, NJ: Erlbaum.

Stein, D. (1997). *Cognitive science and the unconscious.* Washington, DC: American Psychiatric Press.

Stein, M. (1981). The unobjectionable part of the transference. *Journal of the American Psychoanalytic Association 29*, 869–891.

Stern, D. (1985). *The interpersonal world of the infant.* New York: Basic Books.

Stinson, C., & Palmer, S. (1991). Parallel distributed processing models of person schemas and psychopathologies. In M. J. Horowitz (Ed.), *Person schemas and maladaptive interpersonal patterns* (pp. 339–378). Chicago: University of Chicago Press.

Stoller, R. (1968). *Sex and gender, Vol. 1: The transsexual experiment.* New York: Aronson.

Stone, L. (1954). The widening scope of indirations for psychoanalysis. *Journal of the American Psychoanalytic Association 2*, 567–594.

Strauman, T., & Higgins, E. (1987). Automatic activation of self discrepancies and emotional syndromes: When cognitive structures influence affect. *Journal of Personality and Social Psychology 53*, 1004–1014.

Strupp, H. H., & Binder, J. L. (1984). *Psychotherapy in a new key: A guide to time-limited dynamic psychotherapy.* New York: Basic Books.

Strupp, H. H., Hadley, S. W., & Gomes-Schwartz, B. (1977). *Psychotherapy for better or worse: An analysis of the problem of negative effects.* Northvale, NJ: Aronson.

Sullivan, H. S. (1953). *The interpersonal theory of psychiatry.* New York: Norton.

Sulloway, F. (1979). *Freud: Biologist of the mind.* New York: Basic Books.

Thomas, A., & Chess, S. (1977). Evolution of behavior disorders into adolescence. *Annual Progress in Child Psychiatry and Child Development 1977*, 489–497.

Tomkins, S. S. (1962). *Affect, imagery, consciousness, Vol. 1: The positive affects.* New York: Springer-Verlag.

Tulving, E. (1985). Memory and consciousness. *Canadian Psychologist* 26, 1–12.

Turner, J. C., Hogg, M. A., Oakes, P. J., & Reicher, S. D. (1987). *Rediscovering the social group: A self-categorization theory.* New York: Basic Blackwell.

Uleman, J., & Borgs, J. A. (Eds.) (1989). *Unintended thought.* New York: Guilford

Vaillant, G. E. (1992). *Ego mechanisms of defense: In clinical practice and in empirical research.* Washington, DC: American Psychiatric Press.

———. (1993). *The wisdom of ego.* Cambridge, MA: Harvard University Press.

———. (1994). Ego mechanisms of defense and personality psychopathology. *Journal of Abnormal Psychology* 102(1), 44–50.

Van der Kolk, B. A. (1994). The body keeps the score: Memory and the evolving psychobiology of posttraumatic stress. *Harvard Review of Psychiatry* 1(5), 253–265.

Vela-Bueno, A., Soldatos, C. R., & Julius, D. A. (1987). Parasomnias: Sleepwalking, night terrors, and nightmares. *Psychiatric Annals* 17, 465–69.

Viney, T. (1969). Self: The history of a concept. *Journal of the History of Behavioral Sciences 5*, 349–359.

Wallerstein, R. S. (1986). *Forty-two lives in treatment: A study of psychoanalysis and psychotherapy.* New York: Guilford.

———. (1995). Research in psychodynamic therapy. In H. J. Schwartz, E. Bleiberg, & S. Weissman (Eds.), *Psychodynamic concepts in general psychiatry* (pp. 431–456). Washington, DC: American Psychiatric Press.

Wegner, D. M., & Pennebaker, J. W. (Eds.). (1993). *Handbook of mental control.* Englewood Cliffs, NJ: Prentice Hall.

Weiss, E. (1960). *The structure and dynamics of the human mind.* New York: Grune and Stratton.

Weiss, J. (1993). *How psychotherapy works.* New York: Guilford.

Weiss, J., & Sampson, H. (Eds.). (1986). *The psychoanalytic process: Theory, clinical observation and empirical research.* New York: Guilford.

Werner, H. (1957). *Comparative psychology of mental development.* New York: International Universities Press.

Whitmont, E. C. (1969). *The symbolic quest: Basic concept of analytic psychology.* New York: Putnam.

Wiggens, J. S. (1982). Circumplex models of interpersonal behavior in clinical psychology. In P. C. Kendall & J. N. Butchers (Eds.), *Hand-*

book of research methods in clinical psychology (pp. 40–61), New York: Wiley.

Winnicott, D. W. (1955). *The maturational processes and the facilitating environment*. New York: International Universities Press.

———. (1958). The capacity to be alone. *International Journal of Psycho-Analysis 39*, 416–420.

Wolf, E. (1979). Countertransference in disorders of the self. In L. Epstein & A. Feiner (Eds.), *Countertransference* (pp. 445–469). New York: Aronson.

Wurmser, L. (1981). *The mask of shame*. Baltimore: Johns Hopkins Press.

Wylie, R. (1974). *The self-concept*. Lincoln, NE: University of Nebraska Press.

Zajonc, R. B. (1980). Feeling and thinking. *American Psychologist 35*, 151–75.

Zeidner, M., & Endler, N. H. (1995). *Handbook of coping*. New York: Wiley.

Zetzel, E. (1970). The so-called good hysteric. *International Journal of Psychoanalysis 49*, 256–260.

Zilberg, N., Weiss, D., & Horowitz, M. J. (1982). Impact of event scale: A cross-validation study and some empirical evidence. *Journal of Consulting and Clinical Psychology 50*, 407–414.

Znoj, H., Horowitz, M. J., Field, N., Bonanno, G., & Maercker, A. (1998). Emotional regulation: The sense of self-control questionnaire. Manuscript submitted for publication.

Index

References

Abraham, K. ([1924] 1942). A short study of the development of libido, viewed in light of mental disorders. In E. Jones (Ed.), *Selected papers of Karl Abraham*, (pp. 15–90). London: Hogarth.

Abrams, D. (1994). Social self-regulation. *Personality and Social Psychology Bulletin 20*, 473–483.

Ainsworth, M. (1973). The development of infant–mother attachment. In B. Caldwell and H. Ricciute (Eds.), *Review of child development research, No. 3*. Chicago: University of Chicago Press.

Ainsworth, M., Blehar, M., Waters, E., & Wall, S. (1978). *Patterns of attachment: A psychological study of the strange situation*. New York: Basic Books.

Allen, J. G. (1977). Ego states and object relations. *Bulletin of the Menninger Clinic 41*, 522–538.

Allport, G. (1955). *Theories of perception and the concept of structure*. New York: Wiley.

American Psychiatric Association. (1980). *Diagnostic and statistical manual of mental disorders* (3rd ed.). Washington DC:

———. (1994). *Diagnostic and statistical manual of mental disorders* (4th ed.). Washington, DC: Author.

Anderson, C. A. (1983). Abstract and concrete data in the perseverance of social theories: When weak data leads to unshakable beliefs. *Journal of Experimental and Social Psychology 19*, 93–108.

Anderson, J. R. (1983). *The architecture of cognition*. Cambridge, MA: Harvard University Press.